T0407652

If Auschwitz Is Nothing

In memory of Shlomo Venezia,
member of the Auschwitz-Birkenau Sonderkommando
Thessaloniki 1923 – Rome 2012

If Auschwitz Is Nothing
Against Denialism

Donatella Di Cesare

Translated by David Broder

polity

Originally published in Italian as *Se Auschwitz è nulla. Contro il negazionismo*

This work has been translated with the contribution of the Centre for books and reading of the Italian Ministry of Culture.

Polity Press
65 Bridge Street
Cambridge CB2 1UR, UK

Polity Press
111 River Street
Hoboken, NJ 07030, USA

ISBN-13: 978-1-5095-5570-3 – hardback
ISBN-13: 978-1-5095-5571-0 – paperback

A catalogue record for this book is available from the British Library.

Library of Congress Control Number: 2022945472

Typeset in 11 on 13pt Sabon
by Cheshire Typesetting Ltd, Cuddington, Cheshire
Printed and bound in Great Britain by TJ Books Ltd, Padstow, Cornwall

For further information on Polity, visit our website:
politybooks.com

Contents

Preface *page* vii

The New Denialism 1

If Auschwitz Is Nothing 22

1 Annihilation and Denialism 22

2 The Desecrators of Ashes 27

3 In Hitler's Shadow 29

4 'Night and Fog': Erasure in Language 36

5 In the Shallows of Denial 42

6 A Matter of Opinion? 56

7 Technical Expertise and Gas: On the Idolatry of the Real 63

8 The Face of the Asphyxiated: On the Sonderkommando 67

9 '. . . Even the Dead Will Not Be Safe': Memory and Remembrance 73

10 The Future of a Negation 78

11 The Singularity of the Extermination 82
12 Saying Auschwitz 92
Antisemitism in the Twenty-First Century 96

Notes 106
Bibliography 114

Preface

The new edition of this book is the result of my unexpected and traumatic experience of a criminal trial. I was forced to endure this lawsuit because I had termed someone a 'denier' – as I considered quite appropriate – in an article published in *La Lettura*, the weekly cultural supplement of the *Corriere della Sera*, on 22 October 2018. The proceedings before the Tribunale di Milano concluded on 12 January 2021 with my complete acquittal.

What happened to me was perhaps an extreme and glaring example. But it was the result of a pre-emptive intimidation, the product of an increasingly aggressive and devious strategy pursued by the deniers, able to strike at their opponents while themselves evading all censure. Not only did I get justice from the verdict, but it also allowed me to see the depth and resilience of democracy, which can, when necessary, respond in a sharp, decisive manner.

As ever, moments of adversity also represent an opportunity. The trial forced me to reflect once again on the denial of the Shoah, also considering its recent avatars. Hence, the first, never previously published, essay in this volume is entitled 'The New Denialism'. The aim, here, was not just to observe the incessant spread of this denialism and its disturbing intensification. Rather, what is striking is its 21st-century development, in which, although there are some elements of continuity, its conspiratorial matrix has come into view. This confirmed me in the thesis that I had earlier outlined, holding that denialism is not a mere revision of history, or a rhetorical strategy that can be analysed with the tools of sociology and linguistics. Rather, it is a political phenomenon, within which it is important to see the bond of complicity between yesterday's annihilation and today's denialism. This is what I argued in the essay 'If Auschwitz Is Nothing', first published on 12 January 2012 and featured here in an updated version.

Decisive, in the writing of these pages, were my encounters with Shlomo Venezia, whom I had met and got to know along with other witnesses to the Shoah, especially Piero Terracina and Sami Modiano. Of all of them, Shlomo Venezia stood out for his extraordinary charisma, dignity and steadfastness. One instantly got the sense that his story was similar to that of the other survivors, and yet also profoundly different. As a member of the Auschwitz-Birkenau Sonderkommando, he was the absolute witness who, forced to work in Hitler's factories of death, had experienced their machinery from the inside and could prove the existence of the gas chambers and the ovens. He was, in short, the depository of what the Nazis had intended should forever remain a secret. This also made him into a target for the deniers. Shlomo Venezia was well aware that his testimony was the one they most feared. For years and decades, he had kept his silence. He began to speak out in 1992, aware that he was one of the world's very few remaining members of a Sonderkommando. Perhaps he had unconfessed hopes that too simplistic judgements on the so-called 'grey zone' would be revised. But he was stirred from his silence by episodes of antisemitism. He told me that, travelling by bus through a street in the neighbourhood of Rome where we both lived, he had spotted swastikas on the shutters of the shops. He could not believe his eyes – he could not imagine still having to come across these symbols. Soon he came face to face with neo-Nazis and neofascists demonstrating in a square, raising their banners of hatred and attacking passers-by. In the moment, he had to control himself. But once he had got back home, he had no more doubts: it was finally time to bear witness. With his distinctive calm gestures and resolute tone, he weighed his words, carefully touching on the details with rigour and precision. Speaking took a lot out of him – not only for this reason, but also because, as he used to say, 'you never leave the crematorium'; and he had never really returned from that anti-world, where he had been forced to live part of his youth.

Following the publication of the essay 'If Auschwitz Is Nothing', I was threatened by far-right groups and had to live under escort for almost three years. For me, this experience was further proof of the seriousness of this phenomenon, which, given its full import, can only be addressed within a far-reaching philosophical and political framework. During that time, I took part in numerous debates, some concerning the legal question of criminality, on which I had already taken a position that I have reiterated here.

I wrote a third essay which made up the entry on 'Antisemitism' in Treccani's *Lessico del XXI secolo* ('Lexicon of the 21st Century'), published in 2020. It is reprinted here, appended to the other chapters.

The New Denialism

1 Denialism is a form of political propaganda that has spread through public space in recent years. Sinking its clutches into various spheres, it has taken on increasingly insidious and violent notes. So, it would be a mistake to underestimate the significance of denialism: for far from simply having to do with how we interpret the history of the past, its effects also threaten the interpretative community of the future. For examples of this, we need only think of the recent disturbing denials of the pandemic – which were hardly just an extremist, fringe phenomenon – to say nothing of those who mock or belittle the climate emergency. We could mention many other cases. Today, we can speak of a real history of 21st-century denialisms, though this history has yet to be written. In denialism's rejection of the 'official narrative', and in its much-vaunted search for 'alternative information', it offers an insight into the conspiracy-theorist mechanism from which it springs. This is why, in seeking to grasp present-day denialism and its devastating influence, we must consider its connections with the phenomena that have preceded and given it substance – first among them, the powerful myth of the 'world Jewish plot'.

So, while denialism has spread far and wide, it also displays certain continuities. It is closely linked to the Holocaust – it is, in fact, a product of that context. Contrary to what is generally believed, denialism is not some dark residue of the past; rather, it is an unprecedented phenomenon which, since that first appearance, has grown, developed and consolidated itself. We should not imagine denialism's path as a diversion that runs into a dead end, a track that thins out till it disappears entirely. The opposite is true. It is the latest point in a turn which is still getting sharper.

2 If we want to understand how denialism has grown and extended its reach, it is important to distinguish between its different phases. The first of these was the one that had already taken shape towards the end of World War II.

The first to deny the crime were the criminals themselves. A pre-emptive erasure was inscribed within Hitler's annihilation policy. As the conflict drew to a close, the Nazis destroyed the gas chambers at the main extermination camps: Bełżec, Birkenau, Chełmno, Sobibor and Treblinka. The ones at Majdanek and Auschwitz 1 were left partly intact.

The accusations of 'lies', 'fraud' and the 'falsification of history' surfaced already in the immediate post-war years. This same strategy was reproduced everywhere, especially in the places where the crime had been perpetrated or where collaborators had been in no short supply. We are generally led to believe that 1945 represented a watershed moment, a caesura. This is not the case. Persistence prevailed over interruption.

The Europe in which the so-called 'Jewish question' found a 'final solution' – a continent which, with much of its territories now cleansed of Jews, would henceforth be *Judenrein* – did not abandon its past hatred. But antisemitism appeared obsolete, being too closely linked to the genocide. So, it instead persisted in other guises, proliferating behind new masks in order to get around the discredit into which it had fallen and the censure that so impaired its fortunes. It was thus necessary to act as if nothing had happened. Denial provided the supreme means to this end. What had allegedly taken place was – it was said – nothing, or almost nothing; there was no place for the extermination. Here, denialism attempted to nullify the annihilation itself. With this one move, antisemitic Europe could absolve itself of all guilt, opening the way for the new-old forms of hatred that would loom over its future, from anti-Jewishness to anti-Zionism. An accusing finger was pointed at the Jews – it was they, after all, who were spreading the 'tall tales about Auschwitz', and who would have to answer for them.

From the outset, denialism was a cover for antisemitism, a pseudo-scientific shield against all accusations. Mockery, derision and sarcasm came one after another, in a strategy aimed at downplaying, belittling and ultimately denying what had happened. The clear intention in the first phase was to rehabilitate the past by absolving Nazism of all blame, exonerating fascism of any complicity in the murder of Europe's Jews. The only way to make this possible was to erase all trace of the most shameful and abhorrent crime: the industrialized death in the extermination camps.

Over the years and decades, the gas chambers continued to be at the heart of denialism. Once these places had been declared non-existent – the product of an invention, indeed one using the slickest production values – it was possible to write the history of fascism and Nazism in a different way, concealing their 'hardest-to-stomach' episodes: that is, the crimes against humanity. Most importantly, this made it possible to prevent post-Auschwitz Europe from bearing the indelible mark of Zyklon B.

3 To definitively condemn Hitler, it would have been necessary to work through the past. But in 1945, there was no time for that. It was easier to cover up his victory and to conceal what he had really achieved. Instead, the outcome was cast as a total defeat for Hitler, just as complete as

the victory over fascism itself. Thus emerged the political myth of the necessary, inevitable, self-evident defeat of Nazi-Fascism – a myth which is still alive and kicking today. For a democratic Europe that might feel vulnerable to blackmail, its peace at risk of being undermined, the gas chambers were a bothersome detail that concerned the Jews and no one else. Such a detail also had to be considered in the context of the great wartime bloodbath, the millions of dead and the many crimes committed.

But who had really won? And who was really defeated? Soon, these questions led to a first decisive role-reversal. It was the Germans who had turned out to be the losers of the war. Who could doubt it? On closer inspection, the Germans were the victims of an unmerited 'disaster', an abnormal punishment, which compromised Germany's fate by holding it back from the mission to which it was summoned: the defence of Europe and the salvation of the West. The Allies would have to answer before the Court of History for this misdeed of global dimensions, this scandal that so threatened Germany. This wrong risked being passed over in silence, drowned out by the high-flown denunciations of phantom 'crimes' whose seriousness bore no comparison with the real crime that had been committed against the German people. Behind the Allies – occupation forces, be they Russian or American – were the emigrants on their way back, the returning foreigners, the Jews who could now give full vent to their 'revenge'. The Jews were the real winners.

This role-reversal soon became a fait accompli. The Jews were Nazified, while the Germans were Hebraized, in an inversion that would successfully be repeated also in other contexts. The Jews exterminated in the camps were stripped even of their place as victims. There was instead a long-cherished image of 'Germany, pale mother' – a nation which had been violated, occupied, bled out and exhausted, but not definitively defeated, ready to retreat into its autumn years and wait for its moment in history to come round again.

As for the Jews, they were the victors even of this new *bellum judaicum* – and for several reasons. If the extermination was to be considered a real one, it ought to have been completed, down to the last Jew. Yet there were survivors – those who had kept on living, claiming to retell what had happened. So, what tales were they spinning? What slanders had they invented to hurt Germany and cast a shadow over the whole of Europe, passing themselves off as victims? It was suspected that they were exploiting the 'tall tales' about the gas chambers to their own advantage, in order to continue to weave the threads of their domination. In this lay the 'revenge' of these 'hucksters', which was yet to be consummated.

4 Standing at the heart of denialism, the so-called 'Holocaust myth' would already in its early years develop along different paths and with various motivations – or, rather, pseudo-motivations. Precisely because the decisive role of the survivors – the few who returned from the camps – was becoming apparent, their testimony had to be undermined, indeed to the point of hollowing it out entirely.

This pre-emptive annihilation of testimony sought to neutralize all the accusations and to deprive the victims of words, never mind arguments. This is doubtless one of the most repugnant and hateful chapters in the history of denialism. It struck against survivors who had resisted so that they would be able to tell of what had happened, and who devoted their subsequent lives to telling of what had happened, precisely as an act of resistance. But would they be believed? The deniers' repeated blows struck against the camp survivors, who were still haunted by their executioners' mocking warnings, as captured by Primo Levi: 'None of you will be left to bear witness, but even if someone were to survive, the world will not believe him.'[1] Here, too, it is essential to grasp the continuity between the two enterprises – annihilation and denial.

The witness's credibility is, however, undermined not so much by the monstrosity of which they speak, as by the logic of the crime itself. Jean-François Lyotard pointed this out in his book *Le différend*, published in 1983.[2] Some parts of this work drew on the writings of well-known denialists, and Lyotard thus spelled out their basic schema.

Somewhere, extermination camps are said to have been unearthed that no one had ever previously heard of – camps where the crime against humanity, the gassing, supposedly took place. But how could anyone be sure of this? The evidence is scant; in many camps, there is not even a shadow of the gas chambers, and in others there is nothing left but rubble, which has, in any case, often been tampered with. If there is no crime scene, it is only legitimate to doubt whether the crime itself took place.

Unless, that is, there is someone to bear witness to the crime. Here, a perverse logic comes into play. Either the witness has been through the gas chamber, has experienced that mechanism of death on their own body – in which case, they will surely not be able to speak, for they are dead already. Or, if the witness is still alive, they are not credible, and whatever they are spinning a yarn about is clearly no gas chamber. In this logic, the reliability of the witness depends on their being dead; but the dead cannot bear witness.

In other words, the denier will accept, as the only possible proof of the gas chamber, the victim reduced to ashes – whose testimony is itself impossible. If, on the other hand, a survivor speaks about what happened, their testimony is said to be merely bogus. Establishing this underhanded alternative between the witness who does have integrity – the gassed, incinerated one – and the fraudulent one – the survivor – the deniers seem to kill two birds with one stone. For they both shelter the gas chamber from all possible testimony, and undermine the witnesses' reliability. The victims who have not been reduced to nothing, the few unexpected survivors, are condemned to not being believed. Such pseudo-justifications have been repeated for decades.

The denier asks the annihilated to account for their own annihilation. And he tells the survivor: the annihilation did not take place, or else you would surely have been annihilated. Breaking this perverse logic, inherent to the crime itself, becomes an imperative. As it became clear how extraordinarily important individual memories are for reconstructing the Nazi extermination, a wide-ranging reflection developed on the value of testimony, grasped in its full complexity. Reaching far beyond the legal sphere, this reflection occupied historians, philosophers, writers and poets. An inescapable point of reference in this regard is Paul Celan, who summarized the importance of the witness in a famous line of his poem 'Aschenglorie': 'Niemand zeugt für den Zeugen', 'Nobody / bears witness for the / witness.'[3] The witness's word is irreplaceable, their responsibility irrevocable.

The survivor is not called in *supra partes*, as a third party who is meant to corroborate the facts. Rather, the survivors are those who lived beyond, those who are still standing. They are left the task of speaking on behalf of the others who are no more. The survivor's voice echoes the screams of the drowned, the gasps of the dying, the silence of the annihilated. In the survivor's testimony, they survive beyond the ashes; in the survivor's word, they exist for our memory. To bear witness is to translate, to take beyond – in a certain sense, even to generate. The survivor carries the annihilated with them, points to their absence, summons them back to life. It is precisely because the survivor pushes beyond the abyss of nothingness that the deniers so fear what she has to say.

Testimony cannot be taken for an objective proof which imposes its truth all by itself, without any need for the other. The witness's word makes the truth, articulates it by wrenching it from silence and entrusting it to those who listen. The other plays a decisive role. For this reason, testimony cannot be stashed in the archives and, if it is to be and remain testimony, it cannot stop bearing witness. From this stems both its fragility and its strength: it is exposed to every attack, and lacks defences, but it is also irreplaceable by any proofs.

It was the survivors who confronted the wave of deniers. Even with hindsight, we can say that this was an epochal clash, in an 'age of the witness' that was decisive not only for the purposes of historical reconstruction, but also in working through the past. Guides for democratic consciousness who proved able to respond to the extermination by constructing a shared memory, the survivors soon became victims of violent denialist propaganda – not because of simple hate, but rather because of the key role survivors played. The more the witnesses spoke, the more they were attacked, intimidated, mocked and labelled as 'fraudsters' by a denialism that, becoming less preoccupied with the rehabilitation of Nazism and fascism, increasingly tried to pass itself off as a search for the truth.

One emblematic example was Shlomo Venezia, a former member of the Auschwitz-Birkenau Sonderkommando, who had been forced to work at the crematoria in Hitler's workshops of death. His testimony, which arrived with great difficulty in the early 1990s, had the added element that Venezia had seen the apparatus of extermination from inside the gas chambers.[4] Venezia unveiled a secret that the Nazis had wanted to die with the Sonderkommando – and this made him into the deniers' priority target, an exceptional witness whom they greatly feared.

5 As the crime against humanity perpetrated in the extermination camps gradually came to light, there was a growing tendency to deny that it had ever happened. But the exponents of the new antisemitic propaganda tried to pass themselves off as 'revisionists', as if their only intention was to critically review history, to scrutinize it, to reopen the debate, in the name of the dispassionate search for the truth. For a time, they succeeded in breaking down more than one defence barrier, and not only among the community of historians, by peddling their denial as an opinion just like any other, which thus deserved protec-

tion. However, the French historian Henry Rousso drew a line in the sand by coining the term 'denialism', in the bid to circumscribe and counter this phenomenon.[5] This term refers to all those discourses that deny the extermination policy directed against the Jews, and which, exonerating both Germany and the rest of a complicit Europe of all blame, point the finger at the supposed falsifiers, the Jews claimed to have invented the genocide.

Even in the 1950s, there were not many books on the history of World War II – and there were even fewer on the Shoah. One pioneering work was Léon Poliakov's *Harvest of Hate: The Nazi Program for the Destruction of the Jews of Europe*, first published in 1951. As camp survivors began to speak out and historians attempted to reconstruct what had happened, public opinion in Europe and the wider world was completely unprepared to deal with what was coming to light. It lacked the necessary conceptual and emotional resources to cope with such an unimaginable crime.

There was also a lack of precise information. Estimates of the number of people who had been exterminated varied so wildly that it was difficult to form even a rough idea of the massacre. At the Nuremberg trials, former Nazi officer Kurt Gerstein spoke, in his 18 January 1947 deposition, of 25 million victims. Other sources at that time advanced a hypothesis of 9 million. Only years later would the approximate figure of 6 million exterminated Jews be reached. Even today, despite the decades of research and the meticulous collation of data, there is no exact number of victims.

'Did 6 million really die?' With this mocking and insulting question, repeated in countless variants, the deniers' hyperbolic doubt creeps its way in, discrediting and minimizing. If 6 million is an approximate and imprecise figure, then it must be assumed that it has been grossly inflated. It is thus necessary to demystify, to expose the 'fairy tale' that the Jews have been telling for so long. This diminution of the Holocaust, raising question marks over inflated figures, is the beginning of the meticulous work of the denier, who is not interested in ascertaining what happened, but simply in denying it.

It is, therefore, unsurprising that, together with the theme of the gas chambers, the question of 'the number' would become the linchpin of denialism. The difference is that, while the former has been losing prominence in recent years, 'the number' remains the rhetorical argument par excellence, the very paradigm of the new denialist strategy. Even today, it still dominates in the essays, articles and websites where suspicions regarding the genocide are insinuated. This theme can thus also be taken for a clue. There is nothing neutral about lines such as 'the controversy over the numbers exterminated is the only dispute in contemporary historiography that has been criminalised, and it is because of political correctness'. There are many such examples. The apparent objectivity of the number is the pretext which the denier hides behind in order to lend his incursions into the historical field a 'scientific' aura. In fact, Raul Hilberg, in his book *The Destruction of the European Jews* – one of the most authoritative studies on the extermination, first published in 1961 and then re-edited and updated several times – speaks of about 5 million victims.[6] No one will ever know the number that were murdered. But the fact that we do not know each and every one of the exterminated, do not possess the exact figure, does not change the scale of the crime in any way. The denier seeks to force an accounting of the horror and a morbid checking of the minutiae in order to cloud over the enormity of the extermination. The aim is to stop people imagining the pain of the asphyxiated, and to forbid them from putting up resistance against the monstrosity.

6 Denialism presents itself as an ideological hygiene operation, aimed at freeing the present-day horizon of a bogus past – 'the Auschwitz lie'. More and more epithets have built up over time, in a significant escalation from rumour to myth, from fable to fraud. The witnesses are accused

of being forgers; the evidence dismissed as falsehoods and lies.

The Jews are accused of lying. In its successive phases, denialism would clot together around this accusation. It would be no exaggeration to say that this is the leitmotif around which the other themes also wrap themselves. To understand the importance of this accusation, one must remember that it is the cornerstone of antisemitism, stemming from a centuries-old hatred of Jews. In the Third Reich, the very word *Lüge* – lie – was the hallmark of the Jew. Already in modernity, in the aftermath of emancipation, the Jew was seen as the outsider who tried to appear similar, the foreigner passing himself off as autochthonous. A knack for camouflage allowed for this enemy within to assimilate; and he is so difficult to flush out precisely because he pretends to be something he is not, dissembling and deceiving. He declares himself German, but he is nothing but a Jew, capable of corroding and altering a people's identity. For Hitler, who revived this accusation in *Mein Kampf*, lying is a marker of the Jew's existence. If the Jew pretends to be what he is not, this non-being already contains the sentence for his annihilation.

It is thus hardly insignificant that deniers revive the theme of lying, when we consider the profound and serious bond of continuity with the most violent antisemitic traditions. Only those who disregard such a link would ever be prepared to believe that denial is just an opinion like any other.

But why would the Jews lie about genocide? Why would they invent this 'enormous historical lie'? In the second phase of denialism, whose beginning is today usually dated to 1967 – the year of the Six Day War – everything seemed to gain greater definition. Long sought-after answers finally became apparent. The denialist discourse widened its scope and sharpened its tools. It sounded something like this: the Jews had devised the extermination 'lie' not only to blame Europe and blackmail Germany, but also to profit from the 'scam' that authorized the unwarranted creation of the state of Israel, in line with the Jews' policy of global domination. Thus, the theme of the 'world Jewish conspiracy' very soon made its return.

If anyone was still unsure who had really been the winners of World War II, the creation of Israel – threatened and yet victorious – dispelled all doubts.[7] Not only had the extermination never taken place – or else there would have been no survivors – but there were even armed Jews in the Middle East. What uncertainty could there still be? The 'world Jewish conspiracy' had prevailed and the Jews, these impostors, these liars, had managed to fool everyone. The denialist vulgate only changed in this particular sense: if at first the victims of the 'Jewish mystification' were the Germans, in particular on account of the reparations they had to pay, later they were replaced by the Arabs, and then by the Palestinians, victims of the 'real genocide'. The Nazification of the Jews – a people of executioners, perpetrators and occupiers – was achieved through the equation Zionism = racism = Nazism, while Israel became the name for the vilest of scams, the centre of the global intrigues. No one could still deny that the 'alleged gas chambers' of the 'alleged genocide' were a formidable 'historical lie' that allowed the greatest of 'political and financial frauds' – to the benefit of the State of Israel and international Zionism.

7 This interpretative schema was then repeated in intensified form, taking on ever harsher tones during the third phase, when the extermination receded from the historical horizon and the Middle East conflict became the main agenda. The demonization of Israel allowed for a role-reversal: the Jews were now presented as the 'real executioners' of the 'real final solution'.

Denialist propaganda was, in many respects, obscene and repugnant – but it would have remained confined to niche circles, if it had not been for the rapid, unexpected wave of media attention that surged up at the end of the 1970s. The Faurisson affair – the case of the literature lecturer who managed to get a byline in *Le Monde*, where he published the article 'Le problème des chambres à gaz' on 29 December 1978 – was only the tip of the iceberg, and the first sign of the far-reaching, devastating phenomenon that was to come. Thirty years after denialism had first appeared, it achieved an undreamt-of and hitherto unimaginable result. For it was now admitted into the public space and, not infrequently, considered as a simple revision, a review process like any other: the more or less innocent exercise of critique.

The problem concerned the world of historians, and to some degree it overwhelmed them. Directly called into question, they responded to the attacks blow by blow, drawing on the knowledge they had accumulated and making use of documentary evidence. But even the more circumspect among their ranks, capable of addressing public opinion, found themselves caught in a dilemma: either they could refute the falsifiers in open debate, but at the cost of recognizing them as legitimate interlocutors, or else avoid any confrontation, at the cost of giving the charlatans free rein. This same dilemma cropped up everywhere, especially in old Europe, with the beginning of disputes and diatribes which, in hindsight, appear more than questionable. Whatever the outcome was, there is no doubt that a breach had opened up in the defences.

Helped along by their success in gaining the media spotlight, while also enjoying the backing of far-right forces and improbable parts of the Left, in the early 1980s the deniers made their clamorous entrance into public space. Here, not only were they accepted, for a certain time, as historical revisionists, but they often managed to pass themselves off as martyrs for free speech. In a sad paradox, the very historians who set out to dismantle the deniers' intellectual procedures and to expose their rhetorical tricks ended up not only validating the 'revisionist enterprise', but also setting themselves up as champions of an abstract freedom. A case in point is Pierre Vidal-Naquet, the famous author of *Assassins of Memory: Essays on the Denial of the Holocaust*, a collection of essays written between 1980 and 1985. While this did prepare the way for the vanguard of intellectuals, such as the historian Nadine Fresco, who would fight on the anti-denialist frontline for years, when Vidal-Naquet spoke out against any attempt to 'punish the expression of revisionism', he was doing nothing more than recognizing denial as mere opinion. In this view, all that is needed to push back against this phenomenon are intellectual tools, education and culture.

Everywhere, historians belonging to different schools took initiatives and signed appeals. Alongside their fear for 'freedom of research', said to be threatened by possible encroachments, they expressed their firm rejection of a 'legal truth' imposed by the courts. The denier thus appeared as an innocuous critic who only seeks to revise history but clashes with the 'State Truth'.

Underlying this neo-Enlightenment view is the firm belief that the whole problem stems from ignorance or misinformation. Deniers deny because they do not know. This phenomenon should thus be considered an archaic residue of the past, a regurgitation which surely needs countering, but whose scope ought not to be exaggerated. Yet it is worth noting the slippage that takes place here: for an eminently political problem is reduced to an inevitable bauble of the cultural landscape. It is thus termed a 'denial of history' as if it only concerned the proper interpretation of the events that marked the first half of the twentieth century. So, best leave it up to the historians to surmount such unpleasant incidents by restoring the 'scientific truth' that objectively imposes itself.

But the deniers are not ignorant. Also, given recent developments, we can say that it was terribly naïve to believe that denialism could be debunked in this way.[8] Apart from the claim that everything can be entrusted to experts – even at the cost of stripping ordinary citizens of responsibility – the accumulation of data, evidence and information has had no effect. The deniers continue to deny. For they are not interested in researching anything. They make no effort to get to grips with any other reading of the events whose existence they dispute. Rather, they are attack-dogs of thought. They ravenously latch on to details in order to devour them, they pounce on evidence to tear it to shreds. This is how they insinuate their hyperbolic doubt, armed with certainties, which scales down, minimizes and reduces, until reaching their objective: to deny the undeniable extermination.

In this sense, denialism is not an opinion like any other, nor is it a critical vision, a re-vision that ought to be cherished. On closer inspection, it is a political statement which, by threatening the past, undermines the future. In attacking memory, it compromises that bond from which European democracies arose, on the ashes of Auschwitz.

8 Even in the late 1980s, there were still relatively few works reconstructing the Shoah. Especially noteworthy were the books by Léon Poliakov, *Brève histoire du génocide nazi*, and Georges Wellers, *La solution finale et la mythomanie néonazi: l'existence des chambres à gaz et le nombre de victimes*, both published in 1979.[9] Even their titles express the clear intention of responding to the denialist challenge. The belief expressed by Raul Hilberg and other historians, holding that in the end Faurisson and his comrades unintentionally did a service to research by forcing it rapidly to mount a vast labour of documentation, may sound bizarre and excessive.[10] What is for sure is that, between 1990 and 1995, more books and studies on the persecution and extermination of the Jews were published than in all previous decades. History became more and more of a battleground than ever before. The intellectual world mobilized for the academic and media debate.

Yet denialism did not stop in its tracks. Rather, it began its fourth phase. Against all expectations, since the 1990s the cases of denialism have multiplied. Thanks to the complicity of the Internet, the propagandists of hatred and denial have crossed all borders – whether territorial or legislative – gaining new followers and integrating new protagonists into their ranks. As the Iranian case shows, denialism has become a matter of state.

In Europe, the weakness of anti-racist and anti-fascist legislation, unprepared to combat such an unexpected yet already entrenched phenomenon as denialism, soon became apparent. Whatever the polemics of those who defend the freedom of 'revisionist historians' and issue appeals against 'liberticidal laws' – pointing an accusatory finger against 'official truths' – the denial of the crime is almost everywhere recognized as itself a crime. It can be criminalized either by introducing new decrees or by amending and clarifying existing legislation.

The deniers went on trial. Faurisson was convicted in France in 1991; after him, in 1998, it was the turn of Roger Garaudy, another leading exponent of French denialism, defended by Klaus Barbie's lawyer. The charges are themselves important: they ranged from 'complicity in the denial of the crime' to 'incitement to racial hatred and violence'. Yet, as the number of trials increased, with a steady flow of convictions, the deniers' field of action moved from conclaves of historians – where they had never belonged in the first place – to the courtrooms. Strengthened by their solid base on the Internet – that virtual tribune that guarantees anonymity and thus became the epicentre of propaganda – the deniers moved onto the counterattack. They launched defamation suits against the intellectuals, journalists, historians and writers who work on this phenomenon – or, worse, denounce its advance.

The Englishman David Irving, a notorious denier and idol of Nazi skinheads, provided an especially sensational case in point. In 1996, he launched a libel suit against the Canadian historian Deborah Lipstadt, who had three years earlier published a book entitled *Denying the Holocaust: The Growing Assault on Truth and Memory*. The trial ended in 2000 with Lipstadt's acquittal and condemnation of Irving. The 2016 film *Denial* is based on the case.

Yet, even if the verdict was seen to have sent a clear message, this was no isolated case. Rather, the escalation of lawsuits is the result of a strategic choice that the 21st-century deniers have made. For, even as they seek craftier means to evade possible censure, they have also altered the content of their denialism and defined its objectives more precisely.

9 A well-known communicative tactic used by contemporary racism seeks to skirt around the disapproval it encounters by starting with an *excusatio non petita*, which serves as a cover: 'I'm not a racist, but . . .' The same approach is applied to denialism, especially given that it is criminalized. No denier ever admits to being a denier. This is not only because the term is considered a disgraceful insult and unacceptable delegitimization, but also because rejecting in advance any connection with the denial of the crime is itself part of denialism. This makes it a slippery, elusive phenomenon, able to escape observers' conceptual grasp even before it escapes the grasp of the law.

In the foreword which Vidal-Naquet wrote for the republication of his book in 2005, he cites as a particularly striking example of this tactic a statement by Jean-Marie Le Pen, founder of the Front National. In this text read out on television, the product of long ruminations, Le Pen stated: 'I am not saying that gas chambers never existed. I personally have not been able to see them. I have not specifically studied the matter. But I think this is a detail in the history of World War II.'[11] Pierre-André Taguieff revisits this same example in order to highlight the use of apophasis – the rhetorical form through which an argument is asserted through its own negation.[12] The speaker claims to want to pass over a given subject in silence, at the very moment that it is mentioned and thus brought even more sharply into relief. It should thus be no surprise that apophasis is one of the rhetorical tactics most frequently used and abused by a now well-honed denialism, which casts itself as a current of thought persecuted by the law even as it garlands itself in an aura of non-conformism. Indeed, it continues to present itself as an exercise in ideological hygiene, aimed at breaking free from the 'dominant lie'.

But when denialism entered its fifth phase – the one that took form between 2000 and 2020 – it dropped some of its earlier talking points, while clarifying and intensifying others. It did this in continuity with the previous phases, but also with different elements that had not been there before. The question of the gas chambers is no longer relevant, and thus takes a back seat, along with the denial of the historical facts of the past. This development, moreover, confirms that the denialist phenomenon cannot be reduced to a denial of history.

'Who benefits from the Holocaust?' Who profits from it? The new 21st-century denialism congeals around this question. In the firing line are both the 'sacralization of the Holocaust' – said to have become a 'civic religion' – and the so-called 'exploitation' of the extermination for political ends. This move already points to the future of a denialism which is part-theological, part-political: it marks its distance from modern antisemitism, which is too exhausted and widely stigmatized, and yet it continues in the same groove as the most virulent anti-Jewish tradition.

A derogatory judgement of the Old Testament and the reproach against the Jewish God, following the canons of the old replacement theology, are mixed in with arguments in condemnation of Israeli policy. The aversion towards biblical Israel is fused with hatred for present-day Israel. Anti-Jewishness crosses over into anti-Zionism – and vice versa.

The 'cult of the Holocaust' is the pivot of the new denialism. The dispute over the rituals of commemoration – which also embroils the Jewish world, with the criticism of overly sterile ceremonies – for the deniers becomes the pretext for an indictment of the entire remembrance culture. The ambiguous reproach that had been levelled against the 'sacralization of memory' already some decades earlier, has now arrived at its most perverse consequences. The deniers decry the 'memory laws' used to criminalize political opponents. The basic theme is one that had already been in vogue before: the abuse of memory, or, rather, the 'political use of myth'. This is encapsulated in the dismal formula: 'from the exploitation in the camps to the exploitation of the camps'.[13] Masters in emphasizing their own victim status; adept at playing on the so-called 'uniqueness' of Auschwitz, said to mask other much more serious genocides; and experts in the 'extermination industry', with its influence on 'Hollywood ideology' – the Jews are said to have taken advantage of the 'lie' to found the state of Israel.[14]

Although the new denialism follows in the footsteps of this tried-and-tested traditional canon, it also makes a further leap. To consider the 'exploitation of the Shoah' only in economic terms would be to overlook its symbolic-religious value. For the Jews – those 'guardians of memory', those exponents of the 'globalized Levitical priesthood' – are said to have decontextualized Auschwitz and raised it to the status of a 'foundational sacrifice', the fulcrum and alibi of the 'new religion of the Holocaust'. All this supposedly has nothing to do with the 'old monotheistic religion', which – accused, according to stereotype, of being prescriptive, tribal and self-chosen – is thus apparently put to one side. On closer inspection, here the old, well-worn preclusion of Judaism, its content and its history – in an ostentatious, openly proclaimed ignorance – goes hand in hand with the accusation that the Jews have created a secularized religion: the 'Expiatory Cult of the Shoah'.

This 'Holocaust cult' is said to be the ideological foundation not just of one state, but of the New World Order. Here is the lowest common denominator of the 'universal capitalist sacralization', the cornerstone of 'market monotheism', the universal principle of 'Judaeocentrism' that prevailed in the aftermath of World War II. Hence the ban on denying – it is almost as if denial were blasphemy, for it undermines the theological-political pillar that holds up the globalized world: the Shoah. It is not surprising that the new deniers pass themselves off as devotees of 'Holocaustics'.

10 The spiral of conspiratorial thinking is obvious. It is expressed in the repeated associations drawn between the Holocaust and the New World Order. From the latest generation of Hitlerites to the fascists of the third millennium,[15] from ill-concealed racists to Catholic fundamentalists, from Islamist militants to the adepts of Red-Brownism – at the beginning of the twentieth century, deniers explicitly refer to the 'global conspiracy'. The leitmotif of anti-Jewish propaganda is thus taken up in new forms. This proves that denialism is not at all reducible to revisionism – rather, it can only be considered in its full complexity in light of the conspiracy matrix on which it is built.

This was the same framework that re-emerged in the aftermath of 11 September 2001, heralding a new phase of denialism. Those who sneered at the 'extermination fraud' were the same people who believed that they recognized a Mossad hand behind the attacks on the Twin Towers. Denialist clichés mingled with conspiratorial obsessions, pursuing their age-old, well-established alliance. This convergence gave rise to the interpretative schema centred on 'machinations', which was destined to mark the following two decades – and go global.[16]

This schema can be adapted to different historical events and a variety of tension-ridden political contexts, in which – as in the case of the Armenian genocide – denial is a way of perpetuating the oppression. We can thus speak of a plurality of denialisms: the themes of the Shoah are projected onto other scenarios, with new motifs also being grafted on.

But the growth and the strengthening of the galaxy of denialism is above all due to the Internet. The enormous circulation of propaganda passed off as 'alternative information'; the near-simultaneous denialist reaction to events, with its own version to rival 'the official story'; and the anonymity guaranteed even to the most violent manipulators, the prophets of deception – all this is feeding an unprecedented expansion of the denialist conspiracy-sphere.

If its interpretative schema can be adapted, denialism continues to be based on a conspiratorialist framework. Its typical backdrop remains the so-called 'Prague cemetery' – the imaginary gathering place for those who pull the strings and spin the threads of the plot for subjugating the world. When the question is raised – 'who benefits?' – an accusing finger is pointed at those alleged to have invented the 'Auschwitz lie' and exploited it to lay the foundations of the global order.

Unassimilable foreigners, who maintain ties among themselves across borders, even far beyond the Zionist base in Israel, the Jews are accused of spinning a web around the globe. This becomes the super-plot, the mega-plot that works in all the previous ones and stores up all the others to come. To expose the 'caste's' power is to reveal its alienness. The elites are vilified for heading a hidden work of infiltration that undermines, contaminates and manipulates the people's identity. The conspiracy is the Party of Foreigners.[17] The architects of globalization; the organizers of crises and epidemics, of planned uncertainty and permanent threat; the great manoeuvrers who control the press, influence minds and steer politics – are the foreigners to top all foreigners, the Jews, that secret super-society that governs the world's fate. The 'global Jewish conspiracy' is the cornerstone of the new denialism, in its most recent version.

If Auschwitz Is Nothing

> I want to also mention a very difficult subject . . . before you, with complete candour . . . [one which] we will never speak about in public. . . . I am talking about the evacuation of the Jews, the extermination of the Jewish people. . . . 'The Jewish people is being exterminated', every Party member will tell you, 'perfectly clear, it's part of our plans, we're eliminating the Jews, exterminating them.'
>
> Heinrich Himmler, 4 October 1943[1]

> If you no longer recall it, it is because the incineration follows its course and the consummation proceeds from itself, the cinder itself.
>
> Jacques Derrida[2]

1 Annihilation and Denialism

There were gas chambers and crematoria. There was the extermination of the Jews in Europe. The Shoah took place. Its place is not in question. What ought to be in question is the place of those who deny it. For a world in which the existence of the gas chambers is denied is a world that already allows the politics of crime, politics as crime.

More and more people are denying Auschwitz, not only in the old Nazi heartlands of Germany and Austria, but also in many European nations, in the United States and in the Middle East. Denial has taken on international dimensions. Italy is no exception: the adepts of denialism, who have been left almost undisturbed as they have acquired a great following of accomplices and sidekicks, have been building the place for their denial in the favourable shadow offered by recent decades. Hence, they claim the right to publicize what they call the 'Auschwitz lie'.

But what does denialism mean – and why does denialism take aim at Auschwitz, a metonym for 'what happened', a symbol of Nazism's shame, an irreplaceable German name that has supplanted the Polish Oświęcim?

Thus far, the question has been addressed almost exclusively in the terms of historiographical debate. The response to denialism was entrusted to professional historians, tasked with stemming this phenomenon. They, it was supposed, would discredit the deniers, or even bring them to their senses, by presenting documents and evidence and verifying the data. The intention was to dissect the lie, to refute its historical method, to unmask its fantastical accounts, to reveal its argumentative strategies, to expose its alleged logic. The emphasis fell on the *how* of the denial. In what way does the denier deny?

However, this approach, which surely has made decisive contributions, risks being reductive – and indeed misleading. For it does not grasp the phenomenon of denialism in all its complex seriousness and, in following the denier through the meanderings of his perverse arguments, it becomes trapped in an endless spiral. Or, rather, it ends up being forced to prove what happened. The question of the *how* of denial not only means being forced into a defensive attitude, but also has the paradoxical effect of unwittingly accepting and indulging the deniers' imposture. To argue back against the denier, who entrenches himself in the place of his denial, is to grant him legitimacy. Each polemic supposes a relation of reciprocity, it admits that the opposed theses are within the bounds of the legitimate. This a priori equality among rival theses offers the denier the blessing of legitimacy.

The question needs to be taken up a level, from the *how* to the *why*. So, the question should be: why do the deniers deny? Posed today, this question is not only historical, but also political and philosophical in nature. To be more precise, it must be broken down into three different but closely related questions. Who are the deniers? Why do they deny? What is the intention that drives them, the purpose they have in mind?

This is the only way to bring out the connection between annihilation and denialism, which has so far escaped attention. That is, it is the only way to reveal the tight bond of continuity between the extermination executed by the Nazis – through gassing and incineration, in order to make corpses into ashes and send them up in smoke, with a view to a future nothingness – and the denialism of those who deny that this annihilation happened.

But what does it mean to deny? The possibility of denial – a feature of all tongues, which only language is able to materialize – is what makes it possible to speak, and thus to think and argue. If one says of something 'it is not X', one means that it is something else. For example: 'this container is not broken' means that it is something other than broken, for it has been repaired already. Denial is the possibility opened up for otherness, and in this form it must be protected: it indicates a further way of interpretation, it opens up the continuation of dialogue.

This is not the denial practised by deniers. When they say 'it is not so', they mean 'it does not exist'; non-being denies being, annihilates and nullifies it. Their denial arises from nothingness and sinks into nothingness. It is, therefore, a denial that goes beyond legitimate discussion. In its absoluteness, it stands as a system – a systematic, nullifying denial. It is a nihilistic denial in close continuity with the annihilation itself.

Psychoanalysis introduced the term 'disavowal' (*Verleugnung*) to denote a pathological denial, which crosses over into rejection of a reality which has become intolerable. Some have used this to emphasize the abyss of the disavowal put up by the denier. But it would be difficult to reduce his denial to the unconscious, for it is conscious and systematic. The space of denial in which he moves is not even that of criticism mistrust, or suspicion. The denier does not practise methodical scepticism in order to arrive, through hyperbolic doubt, at certainty. Quite the opposite: he is armed with certainty and has elevated his fantasies to dogma.

His is not a mistake, nor a blunder, nor even an illusion. Nor is it ultimately an error. His is not the errant course of someone who sets out in search of truth. With his 'no', he refuses even to enter into the dialogue that runs through – provides the foundation of – public space. He does not walk with others along a common path towards a shared truth. Like every falsifier who proclaims himself a lover of Truth, he forbids it, blocks its way, creates an interdiction against it. He lurks along the barbed wire to deny what happened, to obliterate it from memory, to kill off all recollection of it.

The place where the denialist tries to creep in is one where he can complete the annihilation. This place is at the foundations where the ashes remain. His denial lets rip on what remains of the ashes. It is here, where all trace could vanish, that the master of denial busies himself with completing the Nazis' work. It was no accident that the smoke of incineration was chosen as the ultimate endpoint of Hitler's total war, aiming for a *Judenrein* world that would be 'pure' and 'cleansed of Jews'. For the denier, the incineration in that 'holocaust' was not completed. The fire is still smouldering.

The cinders – the memory of the fire that produced them, which has not stopped burning from within – are already, per se, doomed to burn themselves out, to disintegrate and vanish forever. The cinders preserve the place of the annihilated non-persons, who have disappeared, leaving nothing to hold on to but their irrevocable, often no longer legible, name. The ash stands in remembrance of the non-persons – it is what remains of their grave. But for the denier, the incinerated must be nothing but cinders, a remnant that must no longer remain, a pure grave of nothing. Thus, he denies even the place of the non-persons – he denies that they ever existed.

His denial, his determination to cremate, to incinerate, to disperse in smoke, is countered by the injunction to remember, the debt of recognition, the duty to recall the non-being, the non-presence, the being that is annihilated forever, from the depths, in order to shelter the trace that does remain, which is indecipherable and almost unspoken.

The field of ashes is the place to be preserved against denial. This place, which must be defended, is neither a simulacrum nor a dogma. Rather, it has the vulnerable fragility of that which is, in itself, doomed to dissipation. Jacques Derrida pointed out the difficulty of gathering the word from the cinders, in rebellion against 'the affirmation of fire without place or mourning'.[3] To say that the extermination took place is to recall – as language does – the extremely fragile place that emerged from the abyss of Auschwitz. This does not make it impossible to continue to peer into that abyss with anguish and suffering, with reverence and justice. But to recall the place of the cinders, which stands out from the smoking ruins, is also what makes it possible to take a shared stand in facing up to what happened. To recall and remember this place does not mean placing it beyond all question, sacralizing it, but rather protecting it from the ambiguity of an interrogation – or, rather, of an inquisition. The communities living in Europe today are founded on the site of that abyss, which they cannot erase, except at the cost of falling into it. Rather, they must take it upon their shoulders, as part of a past that is conjugated with the future. In a sense – which is, first of all, a political one – the fact that there were gas chambers and crematoria cannot be a matter of opinion. For this is the vulnerable shared place, the abyss that brings together and founds the community, which thus cannot be called into question.

It is forgotten that Europe has been rebuilt upon the cinders, on this place, fragile and brittle like the pages of the books thrown onto the fires. The ash is the home of Europe's being, of its passing to the future.

2 The Desecrators of Ashes

Even before they pose a problem at the level of linguistics or logic, deniers pose a deontological – and, indeed, ontological – problem: they abolish the real that ought to become part of what is shared in dialogue. The deniers nullify the shared reality, de-realize what happened, undermining the community to the core and striking at its bond. They therefore pose a political problem. It is the depth of this ontological dimension that brings the political dimension to light in all its gravity.

The first deniers were the Nazis themselves. As early as summer 1944, the SS began to erase the traces of their crimes at Auschwitz by burning the registers of the convoys of deportees. In 1945, they blew up the gas chambers and crematoria.

Totalitarian terror operates covertly. This is one of the characteristics that distinguish it from despotism, though the latter is itself a prelude to totalitarianism. The succession of despotic regimes throughout history have put their crimes on display; they achieved submission by putting on a show of terror. The Romans crucified Spartacus' rebel-slave followers along the side of the Appian Way. The Mongols made macabre pyramids out of the severed heads of their enemies. And how can we forget the burnings at the stake of the Inquisition, perverse spectacles that attracted large crowds and were meant to stand as a warning? Even in the modern era, the guillotine did its work unabashedly, in public.

Conversely, the hallmark of totalitarian terror is its bid to erase all trace of itself. Nazism did its work of erasure deliberately, trying to conceal the crime even before it committed it, by burying it between the folds of words. In his speech in Poznań on 6 October 1943, Heinrich Himmler told SS officers – alluding as necessary to the extermination that had just begun – that the 'glorious' page of history that they were about to write had never been, and would never be, committed to paper. Even as he announced it, he was at the same time concerned to erase it. Once that page of history had been written, far from it remaining as a future reminder, it was supposed to be just as gloriously erased. Right from the beginning, erasure was part of the work of extermination.

Nazism did not settle simply for denying the crime. It went as far as to deny that the victims could ever have existed. The annihilation in the present was not enough; it was necessary to work backwards, extending the erasure even into the past. The SS executioners knew that, by destroying the traces of their misdeeds, they would eliminate their victims forever. They would erase not only their existence in the present, but also their existence in that remembrance of the past that would be possible in the future. No one in the future would ever have to know that the Jews had even existed. This was Hitler's project for a *Judenrein* world.

In denying what happened, the deniers are simply pursuing this project. They are vultures circling the fields of death. They feed on what remains of the corpses. They fly over the camps to make sure that the earth has finally closed in and that the smoke has cleared. They return to the extermination sites to complete the crime.

They take up a position along the impervious passage where the grey of ash might clump together and become the black-on-white of writing. Dexterous counterfeiters, they play in the place of loss, in which the absence of non-people has found shelter. They blow on the fire, they rekindle it, to extinguish the words. Wherever a gasp rises from the ashes, they show up to silence it and issue a *Verbot* against it.

They lie, knowing that they are lying, in a hyperbole of lies, as they accuse the other of saying what is not, what does not exist. They falsify, manipulate, distort, not the Truth, but rather words coined with the silence of the ashes. They knock over the urn of language so that nothing remains but the dust. They are forgers of words, gravediggers of testimonies, desecrators of cemeteries. They wilfully trample on the fields of death. They lurk at the edge of the abyss where objects, photos, books, keys, names and reminders are burned. They re-emerge where the fire seems extinguished and the blaze tamed, to launch everywhere their categorical 'no' of fire.

They obstruct the labour of mourning. They mix up the memory, they disarrange the recollection. They pretend, so that it all appears as fiction. They sow confusion and disconcertment so that an event whose reality is almost beyond belief becomes forever unbelievable, improbable, unreal. They strive to stop the story of the non-people and their annihilation from making its way – via the German on all the world's Jewish tongues – into the account of history's losers.

3 In Hitler's Shadow

Who are the deniers? Who are these people who deny that the gas chambers ever existed, who attempt to orchestrate such an enormous lie? They are, first and foremost, the second-, third- and fourth-generation Hitlers. Their 'opinion' is Hitler's truth.

They have built up the place of their denial by taking advantage of an overly defensive attitude – of a story entrusted to testimony, the archives and the work of historians. They have exploited silences and amnesia, the suppressed and the repressed, and an extermination unable to find proper articulation, to be spelt out in clear terms. Borrowing Yosef Hayim Yerushalmi's expression,

Vidal-Naquet called them the 'assassins of memory'.[4] Without doubt, their aim is to deprive humanity of the recollection of what happened – starting from the children of the children of those who experienced the extermination. Yet the expression is reductive. For denial is not only about the past, but also about the future.

For this reason, the issue of denialism cannot be relegated to historiographic debate or interpretative strategies. Rather, it must be placed in its political context. The question of who – who denies? – is connected with the question as to why, and thus with denial's ultimate purpose. For the deniers, the gas chambers did not exist, because they could not exist. But denying the existence of gas chambers means that there could again be gas chambers – and, more than that, that there again *should* be. To deny the extermination is to say that the objective was not realized: that Hitler did his best, but his work was left unfulfilled. The denial of what did take place is the ought-to-be of absolute antisemitism.

Accusers of the victims, defenders of the executioners, the deniers deny that either victims or executioners ever existed. They do so in order to be able to claim that the real executioners are the alleged victims, and the real victims are the alleged executioners. Thus, in their denial, in their reversing of the roles, they can resume the Nazis' work at the point they were forced to stop. And yet they necessarily go further. For even Eichmann never questioned the existence of the gas chambers.

The issue is thus eminently political. The deniers want to offer Hitler a posthumous victory. Having grown up in his shadow, they bring his fantasy into the present, they summon up his political project so that they can bring it to completion. Thus, they deny not only the extermination, but also the project that conceived and realized it.

Against this denial, it must be remembered that there were three stages, determined politically and organized by the state according to the methods of industrial warfare. These are the stages documented and outlined by Hilberg:

the stage of the special status, i.e. of marking and banning; the stage of the rounding up and fencing in, when the ghettos become nothing but hunger and barbed wire; and the stage of transportation and mass murder, of annihilation including even the erasure of all traces in fire, ashes and smoke.[5]

There are those who still speak of the 'madness' of Nazism – often repeating a stock phrase, with a thoughtlessness that is nonetheless insidious. If Nazism was indeed mad, which is to say nonsensical, absurd, senselessly disproportionate, then it is an event that got out of hand, something incomprehensible and indecipherable. Indeed, it is comforting to think that the Third Reich was an interregnum standing outside of history and reason, which thus stands no chance of being repeated. This naive, hasty and reckless view of Nazism has been fuelled by people who had no interest in its project coming to light. Thus, far from being overcome, the politics of Nazism have been able to flourish even in the universities – in Italy no less than in Germany, France and the United States. There, wearing the pseudo-scientific mask of historical studies, the academic Nazis found complicity, an audience and a hearing. From this base, they launched an attack proportional to the slow re-emergence of documents, memories and testimonies.

This also explains why the image of Hitler, itself emblematic of criminal 'madness', has continued to loom over the dark past of the West, with the possibility of straying also elsewhere. It is as if that figure of Evil, which still disquiets and terrifies, could not be confronted in its concrete reality and instead had to be cast into the realm of the monstrously unspeakable. The image of Hitler becomes a phantom, a spectre, a shadow, with the risk that it will suddenly appear again in the present or – just as dangerously – vanish into illusion.

Mein Kampf is not a compendium of ramblings. It contains the outlines of what Emmanuel Levinas, in a short 1934 text, had already called the 'philosophy of Hitlerism'.

In it, Levinas attempted to emphasize the continuity between Hitlerism and German culture, and, moreover, to investigate the philosophical, biological and theological foundations of the political project that was to be largely realized with Nazism.[6]

Levinas begins by speaking of 'philosophy', not of 'madness' or of the anomaly of reason. 'The philosophy of Hitler is simplistic.'[7] The 'wretched phraseology' is driven by primordial forces that harbour a first attitude – a visceral yet already philosophical one – towards reality. A philosophy reduced to the level of 'elementary feelings' – hatred, the Führer would say, is 'the only emotion that does not waver' – Hitlerism prepares for its 'adventure . . . in the world' by questioning the very principles of European civilization. Therein lies its novelty. It totally commits to the body, idolizes it, makes it the receptacle of existence. More than that, it identifies man's existence not in freedom, but in an iron fixation on the body. Biological inheritance is assumed to be historical destiny; the 'mysterious urgings of the blood' become decisive. The authenticity of Germanic man resides in this inescapable 'biological' core. From this derives a 'society based on consanguinity', whose only movement is its own expansion through war, aimed at the annihilation of the other.[8]

What could be further from the message brought to the world by Judaism – the possibility of breaking the chains of nature, the opening of the gateway to history, the exodus to which the freed slaves bore witness? Hitlerism aims its fire against this idea of liberation, taken up by European civilization. The enemy becomes the one who brought this idea into the world, the closest other, the Jew. The rejection of the other gives rise to the need – as had happened before, in the Spain of 1449 – to find in 'blood' the irreparable metaphysical essence to which the Jew must be nailed. 'And then, if race does not exist', writes Levinas, 'one has to invent it.'[9]

Hitler's philosophy is the exaltation of nature and the body, the encomium for the brute fact to which existence is tragically reduced, like a perilous and vacuous sporting endeavour. Also vacuous is the new Germanic man, the future Nazi, the 'Aryan', whose essence resides only in his pure biological being, understood as the supreme political task. In its appeal to the secret nostalgia of the German soul, Hitler's philosophy is a return to paganism, to be understood not so much as ignorance of the one God, but as a radical powerlessness to go beyond the world. For the pagan, the world is solid, well made – or, rather, eternal; he sets his spirits and gods within it. And he models his actions and his destiny on the world within which he is imprisoned. The clash with Israel becomes inevitable and embroils the very principles of European civilization. This threatens all the religious, political and cultural forms that have drawn their freedom from Israel. Hitlerism is neither a momentary adventure nor an ideological accident; and in undermining the idea of freedom on which Europe constituted itself, it promises subjugation, heralding a brutal form of existence. In Levinas's words, steeped in foresight, Hitlerism is an unprecedented attack on 'the very humanity of man'.[10]

Nazi racism also struck against those who represented deviance from within: the people characterized as 'mad', the 'mentally ill', the asocial elements, the homosexuals. In this sense, it is possible to speak of a technical–administrative prefiguration of the Shoah.[11] The Germanic 'mores', inspired by social Darwinism, by natural selection in the struggle for life, exalted harshness, derided all humanitarian ideals, aspired to re-impose the law of the strongest. This would be demonstrated by the measures taken up to 1941.

But Hitler's radical antisemitism, in which religious, racist and nationalistic themes come together, aimed to construct an absolute enemy: the Jew. Right from the start, Hitler's 'struggle' pointed to the Jew as the negative of the 'Aryan' identity which, even before it could be defended, first had to be defined – indeed, invented. The Nordic man, the Germanic man – a myth devoid of historical reality

– exhibits the opposite qualities to the Jew. The emptier that Aryan identity is, the more decisive the Jew's identity becomes. This, moreover, ought to give us cause to reflect on the still looming danger posed by invented identities.

Gold and blood, the sedentary and the nomadic, the forest and the desert, heroism and cowardice, the noble and the unworthy, truth and lies – all these terms were meant to define an opposition that took on the apocalyptic tones of a final clash of truly global scope. For Hitler, what was at stake was world domination, whether at the hands of 'the Jewish plot' or in the universal empire for which the Nazis yearned.[12]

The paradigm is not new and goes back to Christianity. But if, in the Christian apocalypse, Jews must live, only to convert on the Day of Judgement and thus bear witness to the truth of Christianity, in the Hitlerite apocalypse, which is devoid of eschatology and entirely secular, the Jew is no longer needed as a witness to a divine plan and remains only as an enemy to be eliminated. For the 'Aryan' identity to assert itself, it requires the disappearance of the Jewish one.[13]

The struggle against the Jews takes on an unparalleled intensity, reaches existential dimensions. The biological core, a trap with no escape, fuels metaphysical hatred and sharpens the angst – torn between salvation and nothingness – that governs Hitler's apocalyptics. Faced with this alternative, Nazism showed its preference for nothingness – yet this did not simply mean the nihilism of disappointed conservatives, but rather the annihilation of the other, of the Jew that undermines the identity of the 'Aryan' from within.

In *Mein Kampf*, the Jew is the foreigner, the alien, who, in remaining singularly separate, lives among the nations 'parasitically', for he has nothing 'of his own': he has neither quality, nor originality, nor culture; he does not even have a religion, but only a code of practical conduct. The only thing that he does have, that characterizes his being, is his 'lies'.[14] Hitler was not the first to make this accusation. Schopenhauer had already thought of this, and Martin Luther even before him. The latter called for merciless treatment of the Jews, held guilty of secret misdeeds; the Nazi Julius Streicher explicitly referenced Luther from the dock at Nuremburg. Yet, even within this disturbing continuity, Hitler makes lying into the fundamental charge, in the sense that the lie is said to be the very foundation of the Jew, who pretends to be something that he is not. Here lies the point: his being is, on closer inspection, a non-being. As such, it must be denounced, branded and thus condemned to its inescapable fate: that of not existing. Hence, the condemnation to annihilation is already present in the accusation of 'lying'. That is why its adoption by deniers is such a serious matter: in making this accusation, they not only reveal their own connection with Hitler but, in denying that the annihilation ever took place, they reissue the sentence that has yet to be executed.

Hitler's philosophy, which outlines a cosmic scenario, is guided in its totalitarian aspirations by a political project. Antisemitism, at once biological and apocalyptic, culminates in an anti-Zionism whose real scope is usually overlooked. This is not only the stereotype of the conspiracy contained in the Protocols of the Elders of Zion – the tsarist forgery that antisemites still have no qualms about circulating today. The accusation of Jewish lying, in its political version, becomes the accusation that Jews are pretending to be German while continuing to be Jewish, that they pass themselves off as 'natives' even while they remain 'foreigners'. Because of this foreignness, raised to the rank of absolute evil, the Jews are said to have perverted the 2,000-year-old Western civilization and doomed Germany to decadence.

Dispersed and transversal, able to erase borders, and therefore to undermine nations and states, the Jewish people represented a further 'threat' once it began preparing to openly form a Jewish state. Here, moreover, it became clear that the 'special people' is not simply nomadic and, although it is anti-state, it aims everywhere to form an internal counter-power. Hitler takes a stand against a future *Judenstaat*, a 'Jewish state', which, having never been 'delimited in space', will be 'without any frontiers whatsoever' and will topple the world's balance. For the Jew would not be satisfied with a state to inhabit but would see 'the old goal, which was promised to him in ancient times, namely world-rulership'.[15] Zionism is, then, to be taken for the prelude to a 'state of foreigners' in the process of establishing its global control. The extermination is already decreed: for Hitler, the Jews are the obstacle that must be eliminated on the Germanic path to empire. War was the direct consequence of this, and not the other way round. Having established its hold over the various currents of Nazism, Hitler's philosophy found consensus in German society, which accepted the existence of a 'Jewish question' which needed to be solved – or, rather, liquidated – and admitted the need for 'Aryanization', up to and including the annihilation of the Jewish people.

4 'Night and Fog': Erasure in Language

In a scene from Richard Wagner's *Das Rheingold*, Alberich, king of the Nibelungs, disappears by donning a magic helmet and uttering the words 'Nacht und Nebel', 'night and fog'. The Nazis made this their own motto, in reference to the disappearance without trace of their victims. Alain Resnais chose it as the title of his short film, shot at Auschwitz in 1955.

To overlook the role ascribed to language would be to underestimate the power that Nazism exercised. Chasing the mirage of founding a new age, the vocabulary of the Third Reich was supposed to mark a historical caesura. The path to Auschwitz, built in hatred and paved with indifference, was prepared by language.

Before it identified in blood the immutable metaphysical essence that would justify the myth of 'race', antisemitism made its way through language. Hitler himself fomented it. Everything the Jew had was said to be 'borrowed, or rather stolen', starting with his language. 'As long as the Jew has not succeeded in mastering other peoples he is forced to speak their language.' He is a polyglot by political necessity. Speaking French, he passes himself off as French; speaking Italian, he passes himself off as Italian. And he finally had the 'impudence' to pass himself off as German. But 'his command of the language was the sole ground on which he could pretend to be a German'. In truth, he remained a Jew, because it is 'not by the tie of language, but exclusively by the tie of blood that the members of a race are bound together'. For Hitler, here we get to the 'lie' that the 'language of the Jews' represents – a language which he deems 'not an instrument for the expression of [the Jew's] inner thoughts but rather a means of cloaking them'.[16] Hence, the danger represented by the mighty weapon that is the Jewish press.

In his diary dedicated to LTI, the 'Lingua Tertii Imperii', Victor Klemperer, Professor of Philology at Dresden University, noted on 21 March 1933: 'on our university noticeboard there is a lengthy announcement (it is supposed to have been put up on all German university noticeboards): "When a Jew writes German he lies"; in future he is to be forced to label books he publishes in German as "translations from Hebrew"'.[17] This was a warning that came directly from Hitler's own writings. It is not surprising that when Klemperer's book was published in 1947, after the war was over, he chose as his epigraph Franz Rosenzweig's words: 'language is more than blood'.[18]

Klemperer's testimony, a both meticulous and touching account written amidst the atmosphere of everyday persecution, details the overbearing steps taken by a power that imposed its authority by moulding a new language. It makes up part of a now considerable body of studies on Goebbels's propaganda – the rhetoric of consensus, the profusion of slogans and clichés, mechanical repetition and the manipulation of words until they can be put to totalitarian use. Since language is no mere instrument, one can certainly speak of the complicity of the German language. Obscured by the smoke of agitation and charlatanism, dismembered, disfigured and stripped of all dignity, it supported power, whose work it aided even on the other side of the barbed wire. And it proceeded from *Sonderweg* to *Sonderaktion* – from 'special path' to 'special action'. The path that supposedly distinguished Germany's historical mission thus led to the Third Reich proclaimed on 28 February 1933 – that is, to a twelve-year 'state of exception' which allowed for a legalized global civil war – and finally to the 'special action', meaning the physical elimination not of political opponents, but of citizens who could not be integrated into the system.[19] Many were the compounds constructed with the prefix *Sonder-*, 'apart, special', 'extraordinary', 'of exception', which had taken on a negative value. From the state of exception, it arrived at *Sonderbehandlung*, the 'special treatment' reserved first and foremost for the 'special people'.

The German of the Third Reich forgot the refined melody of the poets and the rigorous depth of the philosophers. Instead, it became impoverished, thinned out, uniformized. The word was reduced to a sign. There was a proliferation of acronyms such as SA, SS, NSDAP, KZ, SB, and a boundless spread of compounds made up of multiple words. Abbreviation and elongation were the opposite outcomes of one same monotony, in the service of technical organization. In their common indecipherability, they were functional to erasure. The task entrusted to the Reich's language was to conceal the criminal policy while it still remained a plan to be realized in the future, and to hide the crimes once they had begun to be perpetrated. The 'lie' of which Hitler had accused German-speaking Jews became everyday practice in the German language. This was the strategy pursued in order to reduce the speakers to passivity, to make them accomplices. The imposition of power through language looked to the shout of order, and not to the vocative of dialogue. This meant that each person could limit himself to a mechanical response, ending up as a cog in the machinery operated from above. Emptied of its semantic depth and thus stripped of history, the German language was ready to be manipulated by the totalitarian system and to become an instrument of control, lies and violence.

This marked the triumph of euphemism. Primo Levi pointed out that euphemisms 'served not only to sow illusions among the victims and to prevent defensive reactions: they also served, within the limits of the possible, to prevent public opinion, and even the units of the armed forces who were not themselves directly implicated, from becoming aware of what was happening across the territories occupied by the Third Reich'.[20] The word 'euphemism' comes from the Greek and means 'to say well' – to ensure that, whenever the obscene, the raw, the appalling, does indeed have to be spoken of, it can be watered down or even concealed. The euphemism is nothing but the secret inscribed in language.

Sonderaktion, 'special action', referring to the selection on the unloading ramps, was one of the most successful euphemisms. For, in the semantic emptiness of this word, in its aseptic tone, the crime was concealed – indeed, in a way that would allow for its future, definitive denial. This is what the deniers believe, as they find room for manoeuvre in a diversionary operation already carried out by the Nazis. Yet there is no lack of documentation that makes clear the real meaning of *Sonderaktion*. On 5 September 1942, Dr Kremer, who attended the selections as a doctor, noted: 'today at noon in a *Sonderaktion* from the FLK [concentration camp for Jewish women]. *Muselmänner*. The most horrible of horrors! *Hauptscharführer* Thilo was right when he told me today that we are in the *anus mundi*.'

The pre-emptive erasure of the crime is already evidenced by the word used to summarize Hitler's political project: *Endlösung*, 'final solution'. In the *Wannsee Protokoll*, drafted under Heydrich's supervision on 20 January 1942 – the document determining the 'final solution of the Jewish question in Europe' – we read:

> Under appropriate direction the Jews are to be utilized for work in the East in an expedient manner in the course [*im Zuge*, also 'in the train', 'in the convoy', in the 'smoke duct'] of the final solution. In large (labor) columns, with the sexes separated, Jews capable of work will be moved into these areas as they build roads, during which a large proportion will no doubt drop out through *natural reduction*. The remnant that eventually remains will require suitable treatment [*entsprechend behandeln*]; because it will without doubt represent the most [physically] resistant part, it consists of a natural selection that could, on its release, become the germ-cell of a new Jewish revival.[21]

Night and fog had to envelop language to make all trace of the victims disappear before the misdeeds had even been committed. Acronyms also made up part of this effort. *NN-Aktion*, short for *Nacht-und-Nebel-Aktion*, 'night and fog operation', and *NN-Transport*, 'night and fog transport', denoted the measures directed against persons deemed dangerous to the Reich, who were to be taken away into the night and fog – that is, in secret – and sent to the camps where they would become non-persons. The *NN-Häftlinge* were the 'NN-prisoners', who mysteriously disappeared, of whom nothing was known and nothing was meant to be known ever again. Thus, *NN* meant not only night and fog, but also *nothing*.

From the *Schutzhaft*, the 'preventive arrest', to the transporting of the 'new arrivals', *Zugänge*, into the concentration camp universe, as the crime grew in scale, the euphemisms became ever more numerous. There was the *Empfangszeremonie*, the 'reception ceremony', meaning the beatings and insults reserved for those leaving the wagons; the 'selection'; and the 'showering' and 'bathing' for 'disinfestation', bureaucratically called *Entwesung*, which was to take place in the *Duschkammer*, 'shower room' – that is, in the gas chamber. All this punctuated the phases of extermination and of its deliberate, vile concealment, a double guilt of which the German language bears the stain.

Where the depravity was impossible to get away from, between the gas chamber and the crematorium, the language chose either to slip into bureaucratic terminology or to become an instrument of further offence through cynical, mocking, derisive euphemisms. While gassing was passed off as a hygienic measure – 'disinfestation' – it was more difficult to conceal the crematorium, which was called *Bäckerei*, *Kamin*, *Ofen*, *Feuerstelle* – 'bakery', 'chimney', 'stove', 'hearth'. Various SS documents read B/II/F: *Birkenau Feuerstelle II*.

At Sachsenhausen, the crematorium was called *Station Z* – the last letter of the alphabet denoted the final station. The word 'Himmel', 'sky', recurred in a series of compounds, alluding to the destination of the plumes of smoke which daily darkened the camps' skies. *Himmelfahrtskommandos* were the groups of prisoners who were forced to carry out mass executions and bring the corpses into the crematoria. *Durch den Kamin fliegen* – 'go through the chimney' – was an expression shared by the SS men and prisoners alike.

The language that imposed its violent rule in the camps was the language of the victors. Whoever stayed there longest and became aware of the extermination became a *Geheimnisträger*, a 'bearer of the secret'. They thus became somehow privileged because of the few extra supplies they received, even as they were also condemned to certain elimination. To share in the secret which reigned sovereign in the Reich was to be both rendered complicit and stripped of all hope.

Frenetic and insulting, made up of furiously shouted orders mixed with the barking of dogs: this is how the language of the camp sounded, according to witnesses – the language of the camp that awaited the deportees at the infamous *Rampen*, where the initial selection took place. The intention was to disorientate them through a shock aimed at suddenly changing human beings into *Untermenschen*, into subhuman and dehumanized beings. The transformation was sealed by the replacement of names with numbers. Contempt for the person took grammatical form, through the repeated use of imperatives in the infinitive reducing the subject to a servile accusative. The Nazis had no qualms in speaking of *Menschenmaterial*, 'human material'; of *Schrott*, 'rubbish', a term used for the new arrivals in poor condition. The prisoners were nothing but *Stücke*, spare 'parts' of the infernal machinery.

The Nazis were thinking not only about camouflaging the present, but also about its future erasure. That is what has made the task of today's deniers so simple. All they need is to turn back to the old coded language and repeat it. The *Sonderaktion* is nothing but a 'special action'. Why would anyone think it referred to anything else? *Ausrotten* just means 'to uproot'; *Abladen*, 'to unload'; *Verschicken*, 'to dispatch'; *Ausleihen*, 'to lend'; *Abbuchen*, 'to write off' – that is, to strike a name from the books.

The language of the Third Reich manipulated meanings, bending them and hollowing them out in order to conceal the crime, until they became instruments of power, oppression and death in the camps. Thus, all the deniers need to do is start again from the annihilation of language, denying that the words refer to anything else, and using them – once more – as deadly and funereal esoteric signs. What more damning proof could there be of their link to Nazism?

5 In the Shallows of Denial

The deniers are not a sect. Rather, they form a galaxy that has spread out almost everywhere, from California to Australia, though the old Europe remains its beating heart. Drawing on their solid connections, they make their presence felt on the international scene through a vast quantity of books, periodicals and websites, which they use for their propaganda – far exceeding the narrow academic circles to which they are, or would like to be, affiliated. Looking also at the more recent spread of denialism in radical Islamic movements, and all that revolves around Tehran – where a 'Conference on the Holocaust' was held under Mahmoud

Ahmadinejad's patronage on 11 and 12 December 2006 – it must be admitted that denialism has in recent years become a powerful symbolic machine, which, by denying the extermination of the Jews of yesteryear, threatens the survival of today's Jews. The threat is all the more frightening because of the hollowness of the message – that flat and inane denial repeated obsessively according to the canons of Nazi apologetics.

As Nadine Fresco has observed, the deniers' task is to prove that, instead of the plenitude of the dead that the Jews so noisily claim, there is only the emptiness of a lie of universal dimensions.[22] Upon delving into the shallows of denial – while hoping to escape again as soon as possible – one can only be struck by its extreme intellectual poverty, its crudeness and bad faith. Those who wish to examine this depraved underworld more closely will find pages and pages of a deafening monologue in which the same songsheet – or, rather, the latest adaptation of a score written by others – is repeated in the most varied and phantom forms.

Denial can be summarized as follows: the gas chambers never existed; the extermination never took place. Rather, the Shoah is a 'fairy tale' that the Jews have been telling for decades – a 'myth' carefully constructed to achieve their political and financial ends. The 'conspiracy' is thus the cornerstone of denialism, which, though boasting of its novelty in dismantling myths, is as old as antisemitism itself. Just as the Shoah is said to be an 'artifice', the existence of Jews is said to be 'artificial'. From the very outset, the deniers' target has been the Jewish people, understood in its political form – thus, especially meaning Israel. This explains why the link between annihilation and denial does not stop at reclaiming the past, but extends into a further step which should not go overlooked. The denial of the past, of the gas chambers, serves the denial of the future, that of the 'state of the Jews', an artificial creation which Hitler had already designated as one of the greatest dangers facing the world.

The first publications of a denialist bent began to appear as early as the immediate post-war period. They claimed the pretext of going against the current and denouncing the history supposedly written by the victors. The first to cast doubt on the existence of the death camps was the French fascist Maurice Bardèche. In his 1948 text *Nuremberg ou la Terre promise*, he claimed that the deaths in the camps were mainly caused by the unsanitary conditions, and tried to exonerate the Nazis by asserting, among other things, that Hitler's original plan was to create a 'reservation' for the Jews in the East. Convicted of apologia for war crimes, he was fined and sentenced to one year in prison, of which he served only a few days, and he continued his activity by founding the magazine *La Défense de l'Occident* in 1952. When he died in 1998, Jean-Marie Le Pen, the leader of the National Front, remembered him as 'a prophet of Europe's rebirth'.

But it was Paul Rassinier who marked what can be called – as the title of his 1948 text had it – a *Passage de la Ligne*, or 'Crossing of the Line'.[23] An irritatingly tragic figure, he provides evidence of the formidable glue that antisemitism can provide, capable of binding together opposite political sides. First a communist, then a socialist, Rassinier was interned in 1943 in the concentration camps (not extermination camps), first in Buchenwald and then in Dora; his experience, however, was that of a common prisoner. This did not prevent him from becoming the 'key witness' for the deniers. After downplaying the extermination, Rassinier denied the existence of the gas chambers, starting in 1950 when he published *The Holocaust Story and the Lies of Ulysses*, published in various languages. Through fanciful tales and unlikely hypotheses, Rassinier intensified his denialism over the years, but also vented his rancour through a flourish of antisemitic and anti-Zionist stereotypes. His works found a home in the neofascist publishing house Les Sept Couleurs, directed by Bardèche, which published his 1964 book *The Drama of the European Jews*. Here, it was supposed, the 'drama' was not the Shoah itself, but rather the 'lie' which had been built around it. Rassinier's career reached its end with *Those Responsible for the Second World War*, published in 1967. His name would not deserve mention, were it not for the rediscovery of his work in the 1970s by the publisher La Vieille Taupe. This produced a short-circuit that led to the spread of denialism also in the palaeo-Marxist milieu. Prominent figures involved in publicizing his work included Serge Thion and Pierre Guillaume; the latter, who was increasingly open to the right, did not even shy away from contacts with the Italian group Nuovo Ordine Nazionale and the Movimento Fascismo e Libertà.

In France, however, denialism made headlines thanks to the case of Robert Faurisson. A professor of French literature at the Université Lyon 2, he also tried his hand at history. The escalation represented by his case mainly owed to two factors: the relations Faurisson established abroad, particularly with American deniers; and the academic guise in which he enveloped himself, which not only gave his ramblings a pseudoscientific patina, but also handed him an easy way into the press. Having played the heretic by demystifying and desecrating the hermeneutic tradition in the field of French literature, from Rimbaud to Céline, in order to expose a truth supposedly concealed by the community of interpreters, around the mid-1970s he started looking for frauds and forgeries in documents from World War II.

The decisive step came with Anne Frank's diary, unfortunately a favourite text of the deniers, who – absurd as it may seem – deny its authenticity.[24] The diary is said to have been written by Otto Frank, Anne's father, and by the literary agent Meyer Levin, who produced a manuscript in 1952. As is the case with other similar documents (for instance, the diaries of Etty Hillesum), the originals were cut and altered for publication. This does not detract from the fact that the diaries were written by Anne in the years when she was hiding with her family at 263 Prinsengracht in Amsterdam. In 1980, a Dutch state institute confirmed their authenticity using expert opinion. And yet, ever since the first attack appeared in 1957 in the Swedish magazine *Fria Ord* – coming from an obscure character, the Dane Harald Nielsen – the poison of accusation has spread to Norway, Austria, Germany and even across the Atlantic. Among the American deniers, as among their European counterparts, the texts are said to be a 'fabrication' by Levin. The affront against the diaries, but also against Anne Frank herself, spread on the Internet, where it took on pornographic overtones. On 20 July 2010, the Basel Criminal Court handed down an exemplary conviction, sentencing a leader of the Swiss Nationalist Party who had published an article entitled 'The Lies about Anne Frank' to a 10,800-franc fine.

But the decisive question is, as always: why? The diaries have nothing to do with the gas chambers; they are the account of the long days passed by a teenager who would only later be deported to Bergen Belsen. The vehemence with which the deniers rage against her pages is all too easy to explain: for many readers, they provide a first access to the history of the Shoah, indeed a highly captivating one. To discredit the diaries is to instil doubt that this might all be an invention. Faurisson thus joined the exploits of deniers like Butz and Irving with his 1975 collection *Le journal d'Anne Frank est-il authentique?*, which also appeared in Italian in 2000 with the Genoa publisher Graphos. And he kept revisiting this subject.

However, Faurisson became the object of controversy when, after sending countless letters and articles in which he questioned the accounts of the Shoah by alluding to the 'rumour about Auschwitz', he even got space in *Le Monde*. It published three of his letters between December 1978 and January 1979, followed by his 23 March 1979 article 'Pour un vrai débat sur les "chambres à gaz"'. Showing no equivocation, Faurisson went so far as denying the extermination had taken place. What was new, however, was the reception Faurisson's denial received from the authoritative press outlets, which lent themselves to being his sounding board. This media event forced historians, including Poliakov and Vidal-Naquet, to take a stance, but it also marked a turning point for the deniers, who thus acquired unprecedented visibility. Ever since then, they have been trying to find suitable instruments and opportunities for themselves.

The panorama of American denialism, with which Faurisson soon established contact, is wide and varied. In 1948, Francis Parker Yockey (a pseudonym of Ulick Varange) published *Imperium*. In this work, dedicated to Hitler, he denied the extermination, calling it a 'lie' aimed at provoking a war against the West. Since then there has followed a stream of pamphlets, articles and books – hundreds and thousands of pages repeating that the Shoah did not take place and that everything (even the photographs) was faked. The 'Jewish conspiracy' theory provided the backdrop for an antisemitism that was, perhaps, cruder than elsewhere. The year 1966 saw the publication, again under Rassinier's influence, of Harry Elmer Barnes's work *Revisionism: A Key to Peace* – in fact, a kind of denialist manifesto. David Hoggan followed in his footsteps with *The Myth of the Six Million*, a book whose echoes spread far and wide. It was published in 1968 by the far-right Noontide Press, the object of repeated lawsuits by the Anti-Defamation League. Hoggan's devious line of questioning was then taken up by the Englishman Richard Harwood (a pseudonym of Richard Verrall) in the title of his 1974 pamphlet: *Did Six Million Really Die?* In 1977, Noontide Press also published *The Hoax of the Twentieth Century*, a book by Arthur Butz, Associate Professor of Electrical Engineering at Northwestern University in Evanston. His case is emblematic in at least two respects. In the United States, denialism originated in right-wing racist circles, but through this academic it managed to take on technical–scientific trappings, which doubtless helped it to gain a wider audience both on campus and beyond. Moreover, although Butz faced opposition from students and colleagues who called for his removal, he retained his position. Hence, over time, there developed a certain unease at staunchly defending the principle of freedom of speech, when it was being invoked on behalf of Holocaust deniers.

The key rallying point for American deniers is the Institute for Historical Review (IHR), based in Torrance, California. Founded in 1978 by Willis A. Carto, a well-known Ku Klux Klan leader, who was eventually ousted from the Institute's ranks in 1993, the IHR is a kind of pseudo-academic training ground frequented by all manner of neo-Nazis, deniers and racists. Thanks to the *Journal of Historical Review* and a powerful web of connections, itself reliant on the robust support of neo-Nazi networks, the IHR has helped to disseminate 'revisionist studies' and offered support to European deniers in the USA.

One leading such denier is Englishman David Irving, a failed academic and author of apologetic writings on Hitler. Over the years, an increasingly violent denier of the gas chambers, he has taken a leading role in a series of sensational and inglorious episodes. An idol of Nazi skin-head circles, in a speech to a large audience gathered at the Löwenbräu Halle in Munich on 21 April 1990 he denied the existence of the gas chambers at Auschwitz.[25] After losing the libel suit which he had brought against Deborah Lipstadt in 2000, he nevertheless continued his activities.[26] Convicted in Austria in November 2005, where he served thirteen months in prison – despite being based in the USA – he continued to travel through European countries spreading his propaganda. On 5 September 2009, Irving found space in the Spanish newspaper *El mundo*, to which he gave an interview published alongside others with the renowned historian Ian Kershaw, and Avner Shalev, the director of the Holocaust Museum in Jerusalem. The criticism, which pointed out the risk of putting deniers and historians on the same page, proved all in vain. In his latest macabre stunt, Irving has run guided tours of the extermination camps, for which he has also pocketed considerable sums from his clients. If Auschwitz is a 'lie' created to 'deceive tourists', it is no surprise that denialism can itself become a tourism of lies; if it is permissible to deny, there is nothing to stop even the ashes from being trampled on.

While denialism in other countries is an empty, obsessive repetition of nothingness, Italy's deniers echo this emptiness. Serried around the single leading figure – Carlo Mattogno, considered the boss of the 'holo-demolition firm', who publishes his libels with Edizioni di Ar, the press founded and run by Franco Freda – they have greatly extended their reach via their online presence. There are countless denialist sites, blogs, forums and private profiles on social networks. This is also the case with the US-registered neo-Nazi forum Stormfront, whose logo features a Celtic cross and the text 'White Pride World Wide'. But Italy's Forza Nuova also has its own virtual forum, with celebrations of Benito Mussolini and praise for Ahmedinejad. Antisemitic insults are mixed with the denial of extermination, which can also turn into outright derision and mockery of the camp victims.

A more all-pervasive disturbance owes to the deniers' massive online presence. In a space where an equivalence is drawn between real and virtual, proof and rumour, the reasonable and the absurd, the deniers find inspiration to give their fantasies a concrete form, relevant for the present. It is hardly surprising that the new media have become a powerful channel for their proselytizing.[27]

Although perhaps the most famous names in denialism are French, British and American, its most emblematic location is Germany. Of the many goals Hitler achieved, the most devastating was the definitive elimination of German Jewry.[28] Quite different was the Nazis' own fate. It was not the same everywhere. In the German Democratic Republic, formed in 1949, the purge was apparently radical. But the chance to present itself as the heir to anti-fascism did not prevent it from repeating one of the historical mistakes of the German workers' movement – that is, marginalizing the Jewish question. In 1983, Peter Kirchner, president of the Jewish community in East Berlin, which was under all kinds of pressure and obliged to condemn Zionism, summarized those years as follows: 'In the GDR we live with the consciousness that the Nazis are in the West; in this way we have solved the problem.' The inability to critically re-read the antisemitic past explains why, in the aftermath of reunification, the new *Länder* became the home of neo-Nazis and right-wing populist parties.

In West Germany, in the Federal Republic, built on the rubble of the defeat, the whole issue was at first governed by two key terms: amnesia and amnesty. In the place with the greatest presence of former Nazis, including many criminals, 'denazification' ultimately proved to be a matter of make-believe. In almost all cases – over 95 percent – the defendants were acquitted; there were only 6,479 convictions. The first far-right parties emerged as early as 1945, and indeed they arose in a favourable climate, since in 1947 more than half of all Germans – the same poll repeated a few years later reported even higher figures – considered Hitler to be a great statesman and passed a positive verdict on the Nazi regime, which, they felt, had just been mismanaged. It is also worth noting the rise of relief associations for the Waffen SS, from the *Stahlhelm*, 'Steel Helmets', to the Deutscher Soldaten Bund, 'League of German Soldiers'. Backed up by broad popular support, multiple newspapers and considerable space in the press, former Nazis received a pension and, where age permitted, entered the administrative apparatus of the Federal Republic led by Konrad Adenauer. The Cold War helped to rehabilitate the Nazi past and erase all traces of guilt. A decisive link in the Atlantic Pact, West Germany presented itself as the final bastion of the free and liberal West.

The theory of twin totalitarianisms – establishing a questionable symmetry between Nazism and communism – favoured this repression of memory. It discharged Germans of all political responsibility, and instead counted them among the victims. It was enough to deprive the Jews of this role through reparations, the *Wiedergutmachung*, to absolve themselves of their crimes, to gain legitimacy in the eyes of the world and to silence – as Adenauer put it – the 'great economic power of the Jews'. Collective innocence marked the return to normality. Retreating into the ruins of the cities, intent on resolving the tragedy of the more than 10 million fellow-citizens expelled from the eastern provinces and expropriated by the Red Army, the Germans convinced themselves that they were the only true victims, which the story told by others did not want to acknowledge. Auschwitz was a forbidden name, an unmentionable ghost, a non-event. Having eliminated the Jews from the body of the German nation, there was no one left to remember it. Had Auschwitz taken place? Certainly, it had taken place far away from the Federal Republic, where the vast majority of citizens, who had buried the past through a frenzied reconstruction, declared at the beginning of the 1960s that they did not feel responsible for the extermination and did not hold the Nazi regime guilty of crimes against humanity.

The forgetting was interrupted first by the Eichmann trial in 1961, then by the Frankfurt trials of subsequent years, and above all by the '68er protest movements. But even the – firmly anti-fascist – student revolt failed fully to reflect on the specificity of Nazism, amid deafening silences and stubborn expressions of resentment.

Before denialism entrenched itself behind the label of 'revisionism', it came out into the open in Germany in the form of pamphlets and books such as Emil Aretz's *Hexen-Einmal-Eins einer Lüge einer Lüge* ('The Magic Formula of a Lie') in 1970, and, above all, *Die Auschwitz-Lüge. Ein Erlebnisbericht* ('The Auschwitz Lie: An Account of a Personal Experience'), which Thies Christophersen, a former SS soldier, published with great success in 1973. No lesser was the echo of Heinz Roth's 1973 pamphlet *Warum werden wir Deutschen belogen?* ('Why Are We Germans Lied To?'). This cycle was completed by two books published in 1979, Wilhelm Stäglich's *Der Auschwitz-Mythos. Legende oder Wirklichkeit* ('The Auschwitz Myth: Legend or Reality') and Erich Kern's *Die Tragödie der Juden. Schicksal zwischen Propaganda und Wahrheit* ('The Tragedy of the Jews: A Fate between Propaganda and Truth').

In the mid-1980s, when the name 'extermination' could no longer be made a taboo, there began the so-called *Historikerstreit*, or historians' dispute, in Germany, also involving philosophers, sociologists and journalists.[29] This was neither a scholarly debate nor an opportunity for critical rethinking. The time seemed ripe for a catharsis that would again provide the Germans with a positive national identity. The intention was a political one: to reconcile Germany with its past, through its revision. But this was the context in which it became clear that 'to revise' most often meant 'to deny'. Many Germans ended up identifying with the revisionism insidiously carried out by respectable conservative historians, the holders of professorships, with places in the institutions and a media platform.

The best-known exponent of revisionism was the historian Ernst Nolte, who lit the touchpaper for the dispute with an article in the *Frankfurter Allgemeine Zeitung* on 6 June 1986 entitled: 'The Past that Won't Go Away'. His thesis, repeated in multiple books and essays, can be summarized as follows: if it hadn't been for the gulag, the Nazi concentration camps would never have existed. Nolte claimed that the 'class extermination' paved the way for the 'racial extermination'. Between these two events, there was, he said, a temporal–causal connection. Thus, it was Bolshevik 'Asiatic barbarism' that supposedly triggered the reaction of Germany, which thus decided to eliminate the Jews, the culprits behind communism and the 'destabilizing element' of Europe. In this interpretative framework, the age of totalitarianisms – which are here automatically equated – had been ushered in by the October Revolution. Nazism's history thus had to be revised: for at its centre was not Auschwitz but the struggle against the gulag. In this respect, Hitler's anti-communism necessarily appeared 'justified up to a certain point'.[30]

Many followed Nolte's lead. First among them was the historian Andreas Hillgruber, who drew an equivalence between Jewry's end and the destruction of Greater Germany, which had been defended to the last by the heroism of the Wehrmacht against the 'Red Army's orgy of vengeance'. Similar theses were revived by Joachim Fest, co-editor of the *Frankfurter Allgemeine Zeitung*, and historian Klaus Hildebrand. The polemic had the dual aim of presenting the Nazis as but one chapter in the 'age of tyrants', and denying the singular character of the extermination of the Jews.[31]

It is hardly surprising that Nolte's 'revision' conquered a public space that the deniers have made such efforts to defend using the new technologies. Eventually, Nolte did not hold back even from outright denialism. If already in 1985 Nolte had endorsed the 'Jewish conspiracy' theory, according to which Chaim Weizmann – wrongly labelled president of the World Jewish Congress – had declared war on Hitler, ten years later he alluded to the non-existence of the gas chambers. Countless sites and blogs have drawn on his words. This proves the connection between the academic and militant faces of denialism.

In Italy, the possibility Nolte offered of reading even fascism as a necessary reaction to the communist threat – and thus reintegrating it into national history through a process of self-absolution – explains his success also on these shores. He made countless appearances in Italy. But one that cannot go unmentioned is his 6 May 2003 speech to the Italian Senate on 'European Philosophy and the Future of Europe', in which he equated Bolshevik and Nazi totalitarianism with 'the Zionist state of Israel', which he described as a 'European colonization effort in the heart of Islam'. Invited by Trieste's right-wing council to speak in the city on 9 November 2009 in commemoration of the fall of the Berlin Wall, Nolte faced strong protests by students and democratic organizations. Yet, protected by the police, he was able to speak without disturbances.

Ahmadinejad has often been compared to Hitler. Like any comparison, this too has a certain annoying triviality to it. Yet it does point to an inevitable question: was there a connection between the Nazi extermination project and Islamic denialism? And what affinity could provide its basis?

From autumn 1939 to March 1945, the Nazi regime pushed beyond its usual Eurocentrism as it devoted itself to circulating Arabic-language propaganda through books, printed material, millions of leaflets, and short-wave radio broadcasts. At the same time, Arab and Islamic radicalism came into contact with the machinery of totalitarianism then at work in Hitler's Europe. This bizarre convergence between the crescent and the swastika[32] was dictated by political needs.

From military archives, no longer protected by secrecy, it emerged that, behind the scenes of Rommel's advance, halted at El Alamein, preparations had been set in motion for the annihilation of the Jews of the Middle East and North Africa, in particular the more than 600,000 Jews living in British Mandatory Palestine. To prepare the ground, in 1939 *Mein Kampf* and the *Protocols of the Elders of Zion* were translated into Arabic. But the effect was limited. These were still texts foreign to the Arabic tradition.

However, Haj Amin al-Husseini, the Grand Mufti of Jerusalem, certainly did lend a hand to Nazi propaganda. A tenacious opponent of the 1917 Balfour Declaration, he led the Arab revolt against the British in 1936, and finally, after many reversals, took refuge in Berlin, where he met Hitler. A relationship of mutual admiration developed between the two, also documented in their correspondence. Husseini, who collaborated with Himmler and was aware of the Shoah, helped to give concrete form to the convergence of intent between Nazism and Islamic fundamentalism. This was, indeed, hardly difficult. In a telegram sent to the Grand Mufti on 2 November 1943, Himmler stated: 'From its beginning the National Socialist movement has inscribed the struggle against world Jewry on its banner. Therefore, it has always followed with sympathy the Arabs' battle . . . against the Jewish intruders.' This was how, with a very clever strategy, the Nazis pursued a twofold aim: on the one hand, they tried to propagate a version of antisemitism cleansed of racist elements, in an exclusively anti-Zionist key; on the other hand – also on the strength of oriental studies, in which Germany excelled at the time – they aimed at an interpretation of the Koran that would highlight its anti-Jewish themes. When Nazism gained access to the Islamic cultural world, its propaganda managed to put down firm roots.[33] Throughout the years of the conflict, the Nazis' Arabic-language radio broadcasts were unrelenting in obsessively blaming the Jews for triggering World War II in order to establish the Jewish state and extend their domination over the world.

This is the framework in which, especially from 1948, denial of the Shoah would spread in the Arabic press, where the conspiracy theory was already circulating. In subsequent years, with the outbreak of the Arab–Israeli conflict, denialism also took on extreme tones. However, it was Westerners who fuelled a new wave of denialism that swept across Iran, Syria, Jordan, Lebanon, Egypt, Qatar, Saudi Arabia and Palestine. One of the first to seek new alliances was Zündel, who in his pamphlet *The West, War and Islam* explicitly called on the Islamic countries to provide financial aid to resist the 'Zionist disinformation campaigns . . . about the so-called Holocaust'.

A new chapter of Islamic denialism was opened by Roger Garaudy's book *Les Mythes fondateurs de la politique israélienne*, published in France in 1995 by La Vieille Taupe and by Graphos in Italy the following year. A former Communist who converted first to Catholicism, then to Islam, Garaudy raised the stakes through a formulation that would become famous, speaking of a shift 'from the exploitation in the camps to the exploitation of the camps'. He accused Israel of making 'political use of myth' to legitimize itself in the eyes of world public opinion.

There was uproar over the support that Garaudy received from Abbé Pierre, a highly popular figure. After making emphatic statements in defence of freedom of expression, he had to make a retreat and condemn the falsification of the Shoah. He was nonetheless kicked off the honorary board of the LICRA (International League against Racism and Anti-Semitism), while Cardinal Jean-Marie Lustiger publicly distanced himself from him, as did Bernard Kouchner, co-founder of Médécins sans Frontières. Later, in a TV documentary dedicated to his life, Abbé Pierre declared that he had wanted to support Garaudy, not his book, which he had not even read. However, the scandal around Abbé Pierre, which was soon hushed, was already the tell-tale sign of a wider problem that was about to emerge in the Church: the denialism even within its ranks, such as the repeated and openly exhibited denialism of Bishop Richard N. Williamson, convicted in Germany, by the Regensburg court, on 11 July 2011, after publicly declaring that the gas chambers did not exist.

6 A Matter of Opinion?

The bond of complicity between the Nazis and the deniers makes the concept of opinion problematic. Can it be said that denialism is an opinion? That it ought to be welcomed into democratic discussion? Thus, asserting the deniers' freedom to intervene in the public arena?

In a rather clear-cut alternative between political intervention and cultural response, it was historians, belonging to different currents, who sided 'for freedom of research' against what they called a 'state truth' whose imposition could easily undermine this freedom. The deniers, it was said, would take advantage of this to set themselves up as defenders of freedom of opinion. So, it would supposedly be better to accept living with denialism.

What is for sure is that it is risky to leave everything up to historians. As the bearer of knowledge, the expert is a now-irreplaceable figure, particularly in scientific fields. But if it is in all cases a mistake to leave the final decision up to the experts, in the arena of ethical and political action this has the especially devastating effect of eroding the discursive praxis that guides the choice of common ends. Everyone is tempted to leave the issue up to the specialists, rather than themselves take on responsibility for finding an answer. In the case of history, this would be fatal. For history is not an object to be observed; rather, it is the fabric of our existence, the flow of our lives. We are made of history. For this reason, the Shoah cannot be shouldered by historians' research alone.

Each person therefore ought to reckon with the phenomenon of denialism, even if only a few years ago it did not seem to have taken on major proportions. This, moreover, explains the prevalence of a certain tendency to take individual episodes in isolation, reading them as distasteful incidents which are largely due to ignorance, misinformation and forgetting. But this tendency, rooted even among jurists and politicians, is doubtless coloured by optimism. It is as if the issue boiled down to gaining the 'objective' knowledge of the facts. This implicitly tells us that the deniers deny because they do not know, and that, if they knew, they would not deny. This makes them appear as an archaic and, in many ways, inexplicable residue of the fascism of the past.

Hence the annoyance and embarrassment that arise – but also a sense of impotence – faced with the most recent cases of deniers in the universities, or teaching staff using their professorships to advance denialism. What is the right position to take? What is the proper reaction? Through which channels? If the response is meant to rely on education and culture, how can one refuse a platform to those who would give lectures denying the existence of the gas chambers? Is there not freedom of opinion in every democratic society worthy of the name? Is there not, then, a risk of dangerously trampling on this freedom?

This raises the question of whether denial is, indeed, an opinion. If it is assumed that it is, then obviously the denier should be allowed to share the public space. Unfortunately, however, the deniers want to undermine this shared space itself by opening up the abyss of nothingness. At the edge of this abyss, the question appears in all its complexity.

First it is necessary to consider the effects of accepting denialism as an opinion – or, indeed, an interpretative thesis. Some of them can be illustrated by looking at the emblematic case of Noam Chomsky, an American Jew and internationally renowned linguist engaged in numerous civil rights struggles. As polemic raged in France against Robert Faurisson after his umpteenth denial that the gas chambers had ever existed, Chomsky intervened with the weight of his authority. Openly declaring himself unqualified to pass judgment on the substance of the matter, Chomsky wrote seven pages entitled 'Some Elementary Comments on the Rights of Freedom of Expression'. He was thus taking a stance of principle. 'I have nothing to say here about the work of Robert Faurisson', Chomsky says, 'or his critics, of which I know very little, or about the topics they address, concerning which I have no special knowledge.'[34] No stranger to sorties of this kind, Chomsky on the one hand legitimizes Faurisson, the author of recognized 'work', whom he describes as a 'relatively apolitical liberal', while on the other hand he devalues and undermines Vidal-Naquet's critiques. The latter would speak of the whole affair with understandable bitterness, especially given that Chomsky's text was reproduced as a preface to Faurisson's book, which came out in October 1980, before the linguist could avoid it being instrumentalized in this way.[35] What can be said, faced with a book that denies the extermination of the Jews and boasts a preface by one of the Jewish world's most famous academics?

Chomsky defends freedom of expression in the abstract; he disregards the historical context, the political stakes and, ultimately, even the ethical backdrop. The substance does not interest him; the question of the gas chambers is not his to answer. Perhaps this is because – as he states – he is no specialist. This is all in line with his rationalism, which stands above history; as well as guiding his linguistic studies, it has also inspired his progressive liberalism, tenaciously supported by his faith in the triumph of the Enlightenment. If Chomsky defends the 'elementary rights' which democratic societies have achieved, he does so not only in almost wilful ignorance of what happened in Europe, of the dreadful shadows of Nazism, but also cloaked in a certain 'imperial pride' and aided by the distance he enjoys. From such a position, he can afford to tolerate a few Holocaust deniers on the sidelines.[36]

These ethical-political stakes shine a light on the bankruptcy of an abstract liberalism, and indeed on the limit of the saying attributed to Voltaire, the intolerant theorist of tolerance, also referenced by Chomsky – 'I disapprove of what you say, but I will defend to the death your right to say it.' But what use is this saying if you are calling for my death – and, more importantly, if you are asking me for someone else's death? Evidently, there is an ethical leap, here. And what can be said for this saying, faced with 'paper Eichmanns' who are ready to repeat the offence against the Jewish people?

In fact, on closer inspection, the defence of the principle of freedom of expression does not hold water, either. We need only look at the pages with which Spinoza concludes his *Theologico-Political Treatise*, where he establishes the relationship between freedom of speech and the 'free republic'. While radically defending freedom of judgement from authorities that would otherwise grow violent, Spinoza is careful to point out the possibility of a limit beyond which what is thought, in manifesting itself, breaks the bond of sovereignty and ends up annulling the 'pact' – not so much on account of the judgement itself, but 'as it affects action'. This undermines the foundation of the *res publica*, forcing it to 'ruin' (*Theologico-Political Treatise*, xx, §§ 10–11).

Denialism is not an ornament of contemporary culture. It is not an opinion like any other. Rather, it is the suppression of the conditions for engaging in dialogue. It is a phantasmatic activity, not an intellectual pursuit. As such it is exercised in an empty, ghostly, funereal negation, which for all that is nonetheless fearsome.

So, here, we are not talking about an opinion that clashes with a 'State Truth', for the opinion is itself a mere denial. Moreover, it is not denying a truth, but rather the fragile and indispensable place of sharing. Only if this place, the dialogue that underpins democracy, is protected from the denial that threatens it, is a polyphony of interpretations even possible. Truth is nourished by discordant voices, but not by its negation.

The question becomes eminently hermeneutic. There is no single true interpretation, which stands as dogma, invalidating the other supposedly wrong ones. Rather, one must speak of a right interpretation, which does justice to the event, but also to the text being read and the work being performed. However, 'right' does not mean absolutely right. Otherwise, the doors of the interpretative process would be dogmatically closed. Just as there is no interpretation fixed once and for all, nor can interpretation be a purely arbitrary act. We would never allow a violinist to use a Mozart piece to do whatever they pleased. Differing interpretations remain subject to the criterion of ideal justice, even if this criterion is itself mobile and flexible. This means that it is not possible to simply give carte blanche to individual whim in matters of interpretation.

A good interpreter is one who defers to the 'thing', the 'cause' in question, which has drawn our attention and in which we are always-already implicated. The insight which the interpreter can offer is that of helping the event to come to light, and the text to speak. She is not asked to show an impossible neutrality or to forget her own self. But whoever hides or covers up what is meant to be interpreted is a bad interpreter. This is where arbitrariness makes its nest. If we then move from concealment, through unawareness or incapacity, to intentional denial, then we leave behind the open space of possible interpretations, which sustain the truth, and enter into the monolith of totalitarian logic, reduced to the alternative between nothing and everything.

It is no accident that Faurisson theorizes the unequivocal: in what he interprets, there is 'only one meaning, or none at all'. Needless to say, the only possible meaning is that which coincides with his own interpretation, which is *the* truth. This truth of his, which purports to totalize meaning and seeks an absolute status, not bound by any dialogical constraints, clearly stands in antithesis with other truths, which therefore fall under the realm of falsehoods. In an interview published in 1977 in *Les Nouvelles Littéraires*, entitled 'Je cherche midi à midi', Faurisson called for literary criticism to accept the 'hard law of meaning', just as physicists accept 'the law of gravity'.[37] Applying the scientific paradigm of objectivity to the human world – in itself a dangerous move – serves Faurisson in legitimizing his illegitimate interpretative practice. This is a practice also followed by other deniers that, under the banner of the 'hard law' of a unique and unambiguous sense, silences other voices, closes any further hermeneutic openness, erases any questions, eliminates any whys and wherefores. Is this not the pattern – albeit a paper one – of a totalitarian universe? Primo Levi, detained at Auschwitz, one day asked an inmate why he had brutally snatched an icicle from his hand: '"Warum?" . . . "Hier ist kein warum" (there is no why here)'. And humanity runs aground against the 'why-lessness'.[38]

So, it would be wrong to present the clash with the deniers as a 'conflict of interpretations'. Conflict requires the sharing of language, on which basis it is possible to bring out previously unknown meanings and divergent interpretations. But denial is neither a critical vision nor a re-vision. It is an attempt at annihilation on paper, which continues the real annihilation.

The deniers themselves exploit this notion of a difference of interpretations. Playing with words, they present a clash between the 'revisionists', supposedly ready to revise history, and the so-called 'exterminationists', supposedly driven by the determination to keep the 'lie of the Shoah' alive. To grant themselves legitimacy, they try to pass off the conflict as a debate between different historical schools. It should be pointed out here that to speak of 'revisionists' is itself mistaken, an unfortunate concession to the euphemisms through which deniers seek legitimacy. There are no different currents among the deniers; there are no moderates of denial. Deniers are deniers. Revision is a very different process: it implies re-examination and rethinking, and involves a critical reflection that has nothing to do with denial. The use of the term 'exterminationist' is no less grave, for it already contains an implicit accusation, insinuating that those who take the extermination as the basis of the discussion are thereby mounting an active operation. Thus swapping the sides around, denialism makes the 'exterminationists' appear not only responsible for the extermination, but ready to perpetrate others. This creates the impression that while, on the one side, there are those who only seek a 'revision' of history, on the other are people somehow linked to the extermination – indeed, through a connection that suddenly appears not passive, but active.

Denialism is neither an ornament nor, still less, a critical contribution. The endeavour of those who collect documentation and unmask the deniers' methods and strategies, however, comes up against the emptiness of their repetition and often ends up conferring legitimacy upon them. It should not be forgotten that, for the most part, deniers are not historians, but pseudo-historians who exercise other professions. Historical debate is decisive in consolidating and defending the space in which public opinion is constituted – yet it is doomed to founder when it meets those who persist in denying, even faced with the most overwhelming evidence.

To discuss history with deniers amounts to comforting and reinforcing their place of denial. For it means enlisting them in a shared quest that, on closer inspection, they reject outright, and towards which they manifest open hostility. Denialists do not want to research anything. They do not strive to read events in a different way – indeed, for them, these events never existed. Rather, they obsessively scour the investigations of others to find an inaccuracy, an inconsistency, the glimmer of a contradiction. They are the attack-dogs of thought. They ravenously attach themselves to every detail in order to devour it. With a dialectical turning of the lower case into the upper case, they leverage minutiae to deny the whole. They are ravenous predators who pounce on evidence to tear it to shreds – and to say that it really is only shreds. Their logic is that of all or nothing. Denialism is a totalitarianism of thought.

7 Technical Expertise and Gas: On the Idolatry of the Real

The late 1980s brought a macabre operation that marked a turning point in denial. What could have offered a more apt, incontrovertible and objective denial of the gas chambers' existence than an expert examination of Auschwitz using techno-scientific methods? The deniers' imagination sought the precious support of chemistry, physics and even engineering and technology, to deny the mass extermination using the infamous Zyklon B gas. The so-called *Leuchter Report*, backed by unequivocally neo-Nazi supporters, sprang from this demand.[39]

While exercising his interpretation as he pleases, the denier tries to nail his opponent to the test of fact. He mythologizes the real, makes it an idol, and entrenches himself behind this idolatry, making it the bulwark of his mystification. The phantom 'real', unattainable, unconquerable, and therefore ultimately de-realized, becomes the weapon to demonstrate that all interpretations of that idolatrized real have equal value and dignity – that his is an interpretation like any other. Those who fight the denier with his own weapons, at his own level, replicating detail after detail, in an endless showdown, have fallen – and are still falling – into this trap.

The techno-scientific shift of recent decades ought to come as no surprise. Firstly, because the denier has always tried to peddle the idea that history is a science and should therefore provide objective and universally valid proofs. This conception is useful to the denier for at least two reasons: on the one hand, he can clamour for objective proofs, making a fetish of 'facts' and always invoking that missing detail that supposedly still leaves everything beyond the bounds of credibility; on the other hand, he in turn garlands himself with an aura of science, chancing his hand as an expert in order to deny that the extermination took place.

Where to start? Obviously from the place that has to be denied – meaning the site of the Auschwitz gas chambers. Once that place has been taken out of the picture, once that disgrace has been washed away, it is possible to move on to 'revise' everything else. Above all, it is possible to tacitly rehabilitate Hitlerism. The floor is therefore given to the experts – supposedly engineers and chemists – to dismantle the remains of the gas chambers and crematoria.

A US expert on electric chairs, execution devices and gas chambers, Fred A. Leuchter was hired in 1988 by the defence team of Ernst Zündel, a German writer and publisher who turned a profit in Toronto by disseminating publications that denied the extermination. After Auschwitz survivor Sabine Citron filed a complaint against him in 1985, Zündel was brought before the District Court and sentenced in the first instance to five months in prison; but the Ontario Court of Appeal overturned this verdict in 1987 and ordered a new trial. The network of deniers which operated around Zündel found valuable help in both Faurisson and Irving, who got in touch with Leuchter and asked him to draw up an expert report proving that extermination by gas could not have taken place at Auschwitz.

Having embraced the denialist cause – and pocketed $35,000 from Zündel – Leuchter made haste to prove the technical impossibility of mass gassings. The fake engineer flew to Poland on 25 February 1988, accompanied by his wife and a team of helpers, including a draughtsman, a cameraman and an interpreter. He inspected the area of the former Auschwitz and Majdanek camps. During his three-day inspection – and despite lacking any authorization – he used a chisel to take samples from the ruins of the crematoria, to be taken home for chemical analysis. On 3 March, he returned to Boston and, with similar speed, drew up the 132-page report, which was already finished by 5 April. Deemed entirely irrelevant by the Toronto court, it nevertheless aroused enthusiasm in denialist circles, who saw the *Leuchter Report* as a milestone – the definitive proof that the gas chambers never existed.

While Leuchter passed off his report as an independent, neutral analysis conducted using scientific methods, he had merely sought to credit and reinforce the old denialist slogan, coined by Louis Darquier de Pellepoix, that 'only fleas were gassed in Auschwitz'.[40] Thus, the key question was the use of Zyklon B, which was poured into the chambers once the doors were sealed. Leuchter denies that extermination could have taken place in the buildings at Auschwitz, because the 'alleged' gas chambers could not be quickly heated and ventilated. He sarcastically remarks that '[i]t seems unusual that the presumed designers of these alleged gas chambers never consulted or considered the United States technology; the only country then executing prisoners with gas'.[41] But Leuchter's sensational discovery is that the blue stains of hydrogen cyanide on the samples taken from the walls of the former gas chambers are 'barely visible'. Far stronger, however, are the traces left on the walls of the disinfection rooms. Chemical analyses confirm this. It follows, for Leuchter, that Zyklon B was only used as a pesticide and that the gas chambers never existed.

One response came from the biochemist Georges Wellers – a survivor of the extermination and author of a demolition of the report, published in the *Dachauer Hefte*. As Wellers observes, not only does Leuchter somehow find it strange that between 1941 and 1942, at the height of the war, the camp commander Rudolf Höß did not turn to US experts for information about their well-known – indeed, tried-and-tested – facilities, but moreover he 'confuses his

Hilton Hotel gas chambers with the miserable barns of Auschwitz'.[42] Since hydrogen cyanide passes into the aeriform state at around 26 degrees Celsius, the chambers were pre-heated in US prisons where, for 'humanitarian' reasons, the gas introduced was eleven times the lethal dose. At Auschwitz, the Nazis brutally packed a chamber with hundreds of naked, terrified, screaming people crowding into each other. Gasping for air, they ended up rapidly breathing in the Zyklon B, which had turned into gas on account of the heat of the human body. Even though the dose was smaller here, they took in greater quantities of it. As some witnesses have testified, this did not stop some cases of prisoners surviving by lying flat on the floor – especially children.

The *Leuchter Report* was debunked by the French toxicologist Jean-Claude Pressac, who published *Auschwitz: Technique and Operation of the Gas Chambers* in 1989. Added to that were the findings of his further investigations, based on documents that emerged from the Moscow archives, themselves collected in the volume *Les Crématoires d'Auschwitz: la machinerie du meurtre de masse*. Pressac clarified, among other things, that while disinfestation took hours and required a higher concentration of pesticide, the gassing of people took only 10 to 12 minutes and a smaller quantity of Zyklon B. Insects have more resistance to it than human beings. It is thus unsurprising that the remains of the rooms used for disinfection bore heavier traces of cyanides. Moreover, Leuchter need only have considered the report released on 15 December 1945 by the Institute of Forensic Medicine in Krakow, which analysed a 25.5 kg sample of the 293 bags of women's hair found in the storerooms at Auschwitz, and established the unequivocal presence of traces of hydrogen cyanide.

A third scientific demolition of the *Leuchter Report* came in a detailed study by Werner Wegner. He forcefully insisted on the need to counter this 'field survey' with scientific demonstrations, even where its depravity and extravagance are apparent.[43] For Wegner, political-ethical arguments risked making those who preferred to avoid engagement look like they had a weak point.

What is for sure is that, notwithstanding all the rebuttals, for deniers the *Leuchter Report* has continued to serve as definitive proof that the gas chambers never existed. Published in numerous languages, it swaggered through the 1990s, becoming a keystone of a radical right which exploited it for propaganda.

In Germany, the *Leuchter Report* has had devastating effects. Supported by further field surveys, such as the one which the Nazi general Otto E. Remer commissioned from the chemist Germar Rudolf – later convicted of denialism – it even sparked a heated polemic in which Ernst Nolte intervened, publicly defending the report and endorsing its scientific character. In a 1994 interview with weekly magazine *Der Spiegel*, he averred: 'I cannot dismiss the importance of the investigation into the traces of hydrogen cyanide in the gas chambers, which was first undertaken by the American engineer [!] Fred Leuchter.'

8 The Face of the Asphyxiated: On the Sonderkommando

Technical evidence and scientific proofs do not silence the deniers. Faced with corroborations, rebuttals and refutations, they pursue the same strategy: they shield themselves behind their own certainties, while also trying to creep into those spaces that even scientific demonstration inevitably leaves open, in order to raise further objections and sow new poisonous doubts.

Those who think that history will show the 'objective' truth certainly do not get the better of the deniers – rather, they end up falling into a trap, as they are forced into micro-analysing the detail: from the exact amount of Zyklon B poured into the chambers, to the number of minutes and seconds the gassing took, to the tally of corpses burned each day in the ovens.

In this accounting of horror, every slightest inaccuracy is a source of scrutiny and sharp critique. It seems, then, that pseudo-scientific denialism does not only pursue the unattainable goal of demonstrating the technical impossibility of the Shoah. Behind this aspiration lies another, more insidious and terrible one. Denial forces a checking of minutiae, an examination of particulars, in an investigation that gets lost in the details. This means losing sight of the sheer enormity of what we are talking about. Is this not the real intention? To hermetically seal the iron doors of the gas chambers? To leave behind the muffled screams? To ensure that our gaze never meets with the unseeing eyes of the asphyxiated?

The aim is to make us accomplices. The inadequacy of our feeling and imagining, faced with something beyond all measure, leaves us indifferent. We become emotionally illiterate: 6 million is just a number. And while we count that endless tally in vain, as we inadvertently delve into debate about the non-being of millions, we no longer feel the horror, we no longer feel pity and compassion, we no longer feel responsibility. Because responsibility also has to do with imagination. We cannot imagine the distress of those who waited, the pain of the asphyxiated, the sufferings of the burned and half-burned. We are prevented from doing so by the denier, who has on his side what Günther Anders called the 'infernal rule' – the impotence of our imagination, so fruitfully exploited by Eichmann.[44] We are also prevented from doing what Eichmann could not do – indeed, had to not allow himself to do – that is, to meet the gaze of the asphyxiated. In this way, we are barred from putting up resistance to the monstrosity.

The deniers' continuity with the Nazis thus again comes into view. Caught up in their specialized tasks, carried out with exacting diligence, the Nazis remained distant from the end result of their actions. The enormity of that outcome made them incapable of imagining it. This indirect connection between their work and its product made the whole endeavour simpler, for it left them indifferent to the 'human material' that they were working so hard to eliminate. They easily averted their gaze, escaping the terrible face-to-face encounter between victim and executioner. In Hitler's workshops of death, the murder of the nameless was officiated over anonymously. Thus, the responsibility was erased, even before the crime itself. Who would answer for all this? Those who led the victims into the gas chambers? Those who poured in the Zyklon B? Those who incinerated them? But these intermediate tasks were assigned to the members of the Sonderkommandos, who were condemned to an immediate relationship with death.

Similarly, the 'paper Eichmanns' distract and turn our gaze away from the industrial extermination of human lives, while everything is belittled and anatomized. In this macabre exercise, the non-persons, turned into numbers and objects, are annihilated once more. At the border station, at the inescapable crossroads, between attention and indifference, responsibility and ruthlessness, the deniers urge us to retread the path of gassing and cremation adopting their own attitude – the attitude of the executioners.

So, let's delve into the denied place, the place of the gas chambers and crematoria, through the testimony of Shlomo Venezia. His account is all the more valuable because, according to the deniers, no victim ever gave eyewitness testimony about a gassing. An Italian Jew, born and raised in Thessaloniki, Shlomo Venezia was arrested with his family in Athens and arrived at Auschwitz-Birkenau on 11 April 1944. There, after an initial selection, he was 'injected' with the number 182727. One of the very few surviving members of the Sonderkommando, for years he kept his silence. His testimony, collected in the book *Inside the Gas Chambers*, is not only significant because it offers overwhelming proof, an attestation against the denial. It is this, but also much more than that. Several historians have acknowledged that they understood what the concentration camps were only once they had read the survivors' accounts. It is as if leafing through documents was not enough. Vidal-Naquet attributes this to an 'irrational component' within the historian's work, as in his own life. Yet this is not a matter of irrationality. The testimony of Shlomo Venezia, who lived in the realm between the gas chamber and the crematorium, narrates the human encounter that took place amidst the extreme dehumanization, thus giving the asphyxiated their faces back.

Venezia describes his first confrontation with the erasure inscribed in the word 'Sonderkommando':

> he told me we were in the 'Sonderkommando'.
> 'What does "Sonderkommando" mean?'
> 'Special detachment.'
> 'Special. Why?'
> 'Because you have to work in the Crematorium . . . where the people are burned.'
> . . .
> But it didn't take me long to realize that we had been incorporated into the Sonderkommando to replace former prisoners who had been 'selected' and killed.[45]

And he recounts the different stages of annihilation, right up to incineration, without failing to mention the denial of the crime that made it possible in the first place.

> Every time a new convoy arrived, people went in through the big door of the Crematorium and were directed towards the underground staircase that led to the undressing room. There were so many of them that we saw the queue stretching out like a long snake. As the first of them were entering, the last were still a hundred yards or so behind. After the selection on the ramp, the women, children, and old men were sent in first, then the other men arrived. In the undressing room, there were coat hooks with numbers all along the wall, as well as little wooden planks on which people could sit to get undressed. To deceive them more effectively, the Germans told people to pay particular attention to the numbers, so that they'd be able to find their things more easily when they came out of the 'shower.' . . . These instructions were generally given by the SS stand-

ing guard, but it sometimes happened that a man in the Sonderkommando could speak the language of the deportees and transmit these instructions to them directly. To calm people down and ensure they'd go through more quickly, without making any fuss, the Germans also promised them they'd have a meal just after 'disinfection'. Many of the women hurried up so as to be first in line and get it all over with as quickly as possible – especially as the children were terrified and clung to their mothers. For them, even more than for the others, everything must have been strange, eerie, dark, cold.

Once they had taken off their clothes, the women went into the gas chamber and waited, thinking that they were in a shower, with the shower heads hanging over them. They couldn't know where they really were. . . . Then the men, too, were finally pushed into the gas chamber. The Germans thought that if they made thirty or so strong men go in last, they would be able, with their force, to push the others right in. And indeed, herded by the rain of blows as if they were so many animals, their only option was to push hard to get into the room to avoid the beating. That's why I think that many of them were dead or dying even before the gas was released. . . . Then, finally, the German bringing the gas would arrive. It took two prisoners from the Sonderkommando to help him lift up the external trapdoor, above the gas chamber, then he introduced Zyklon B through the opening. The lid was made of very heavy cement. The German would never have bothered to lift it up himself, as it needed two of us. Sometimes it was me, sometimes others. . . . The cover was just opened, the gas thrown in, and the cover closed again. But the German merely threw the gas in; it wasn't even he who opened or closed. Once the gas had been thrown in, it lasted about ten to twelve minutes, then finally you couldn't hear anything anymore, not a living soul. A German came to check that everyone was really dead by looking through a peephole placed in the thick door . . . When he was sure that everyone was well and truly dead, he opened the door and came out right away, after starting the ventilation system. For twenty minutes, you could hear a loud throbbing noise, like a machine breathing in air. Then, finally, we could go in and start to bring the corpses out of the gas chamber. A terrible, acrid smell filled the room. We couldn't distinguish between what came from the specific smell of the gas and what came from the smell of the people and the human excrement.

. . .

I was given scissors and had to cut off the women's hair. I just cut off the longest hair, and didn't touch the men. Especially useful were the long tresses, easy to cut off and transport. Both hands were needed to cut with those big pairs of scissors. Then the hair was picked up and put into a big sack. At regular intervals, a truck came to pick up the sacks of hair that had been set to one side so as to convey them to a place in town where they were stored.

When the job of cutting the hair and pulling out the gold teeth had been completed, two people came to take the bodies and to load them onto the hoist that sent them up to the ground floor of the building, and the Crematorium ovens . . . The bodies were then dragged and laid out in front of the ovens, two by two. In front of every muffle, three men were waiting to place the bodies in the oven. The bodies were laid out head to foot on a kind of stretcher. Two men, either side of the stretcher, lifted it with the help of a long piece of wood slipped underneath it. The third man, facing the ovens, held the handles that were used to push the stretcher into the furnace. They had to slip the bodies in and pull the stretcher out quickly, before the iron grew too hot. The men in the Sonderkommando had got into the habit of pouring water onto the stretcher before disposing of the bodies, otherwise these remained stuck to the red-hot iron. In cases such as that, the work became very difficult, since the bodies had to be pulled out with a fork and pieces of skin remained attached. When this happened, the whole process was slowed down and the Germans could accuse us of sabotage. So we had to move quickly and skillfully. . . .

Once the room had been emptied, it had to be thoroughly cleaned, since the walls and the floor were all dirty, and it was impossible to get new people in without their panicking at the sight of the traces of blood and all the rest on the walls and on the ground. We first had to clean the floor, wait for it to dry and then whitewash the walls. The venti-

> lator continued to clean the air. Thus, everything was ready for the arrival of a new group. Even if people saw the floor was wet when they came in, this didn't strike them as being suspicious, since they'd been told that they'd be going into the shower to be disinfected.
>
> . . .
>
> The ashes had to be eliminated too, so as to leave no trace. In fact, certain bones, those of the pelvis, for instance, didn't burn very well, either in the ovens or, indeed, in the ditches. That's why the thickest bones had to be taken out and ground up separately, before being mixed with the ashes. The operation took place in the Crematorium yard, behind the building. In Crematorium III, for example, the place where the bones were ground was in the corner next to the hospital and the Gypsy camp. Once the ashes had all been ground up, they were transported on the back of a little wagon. At regular intervals, a truck came to collect them so they could be thrown into the river.[46]

9 '. . . Even the Dead Will Not Be Safe': Memory and Remembrance

Denialism has always raged against memory. It has thus sought to demolish the testimony of survivors, whose accounts are said to be false, distorted, invented. The denialist mobilization against memory is underestimated. The clash, which is still under way, has an epochal depth: on the one hand, the exaltation of forgetting, in its pagan echoes; on the other, the Jewish injunction *zakhòr*, 'remember!' On the one hand, the deniers' unanimity in invoking a 'yes to forgetting', to that fading away which is understood as a characteristic of human memory; on the other hand, the yearning of the survivors who – clinging to the bond between remembrance, testimony and writing – have tried to rise from the bottom of the abyss by handing down their accounts to others and to themselves. They have done so not only out of their own individual need, but to share their remembrance, to entrust it to the community.

With his typical insight, Primo Levi wrote that 'the entire history of the short-lived "thousand-year Reich" can be re-read as a war against memory'.[47] The erasure of the crime in language was already a prelude to the abuse of memory. Levi was aware that this could be avoided only through vigilance, sustained and substantiated by bearing witness. This is why memory is the pivot around which his work revolves. 'We hoped not to live *and* tell, but to live *to* tell.'[48]

As denialism has intensified and extended its reach, the attacks on memory have multiplied. On 11 October 1998, the writer Martin Walser, who was awarded the prestigious 'Booksellers' Peace Prize' in Frankfurt, took the opportunity to declare the 'uselessness of remembering Auschwitz', which, if 'instrumentalized', would end up hanging over the German nation like a moralistic sword of Damocles. The immediate retort from Ignaz Bubis, the then-president of the Jüdischer Zentralrat (Jewish Central Council), who called the speech a 'mental pyre', remained isolated. Such episodes have recurred also elsewhere, and a current has emerged which, providing defences of forgetting, warns against falling into what Paul Ricœur calls 'the trap of the duty of remembrance', whose abuses it denounces.[49] This current, which clearly crosses political divides, has fed the development of an outright 'critique of memory', which seems to want to compete with the critique of reason. This is perhaps unprecedented in the history of thought. Why all this fuss about memory?

To begin with, memory is said to be 'saturated', as Régine Robin puts it, giving voice to an ill-concealed impatience towards a chapter of the past that ought to have been closed long ago, sealed by some absolutory pardon.[50] Once it has been observed that memory is saturated already, it is then easy to point the finger at those who seem to have a 'special calling' for it – that is, the Jews who, obsessed with the cult of memory, would like to impose their duty on others, while retaining the monopoly by which they set themselves up as 'guardians of the temple'. Made the object of 'commemoration and lament' and removed from the domain of 'critical thinking', memory – Peter Novick claims – ends up becoming a 'civil religion', with its own icons, dogmas and rituals, all of which are untouchable.[51] The next step is the accusation of the 'political use of memory', instrumentalized to achieve present-day objectives. The chorus of critics of memory has Israel in its sights.

There is no shortage of those who, with a touch of condescension, say that the memory of the crime is 'useless'. But the writings that criticize memory as reified kitsch are themselves mostly just as kitsch, and on closer inspection prove specious. Obviously, memory steers a course between both sacralization and trivialization, two rocks which it risks foundering against. Has the 'day of remembrance' not become a sloganistic way of creating all manner of anniversaries almost every day of the year? This does not, however, mean that 'commemoration' has a negative meaning, as some would insinuate. This reflects the advance of the quasi-philosophical argument holding that memory is an individual matter, whereas 'collective memory' is a confection – a paradox intrinsic to the Jewish injunction to remembrance, which is thus called into question. If one makes a duty of memory, which springs from subjective perception, does that not mean imposing it in an 'objective' form which takes on the status of a myth? This question also runs through Avishai Margalit's book *The Ethics of Memory*, albeit without finding an answer.[52]

Yet, on this point, it is enough to turn back to the Jewish tradition, where remembrance is indeed a *mitzvah*, an obligation. Remembering is not just a dominant theme – rather, it is the very condition of the Torah and its narration. The verb *zakhàr*, in its various forms, inspires the verses, underpins the text, recurs countless times. Remembrance is fulfilled through the narration of the past; Judaism thus introduced the concept of 'history', which would become a universal heritage. But remembrance does not stop at the telling of the story; rather, it remains the obligation around which the community is built, the precept that has the power to unite and hold the Jewish people together. For this reason, remembrance cannot be experienced as a contingent event. One belongs to Israel insofar as one lives by observing the imperative: *zakhòr*, 'remember!' On the other hand, it is thanks to remembrance that Israel has survived.

But it is, indeed, necessary to distinguish between memory and remembrance. If memory is instinctive and unreflective, left up to the spontaneity of the individual, in whom it also risks vanishing without trace, remembrance is the task of the community that constitutes itself by observing remembrance in the present. One remembers by observing, one observes by remembering. The imperative *shamór*, 'observe', comes later; it is addressed to those who did not live through the events and can have no memory of them, but bear the responsibility of keeping alive the remembrance of them, through its observance. In this sense, the question raised by the end of the 'age of the witness' loses its significance. To practise remembrance is to recall the past in the present, with a view to the future. Telling the story, which maintains the remembrance of the past event in words, opens up the possibility of commemoration, of sharing in memory, of participating in the community. Telling the story is already a redemption; history is already a reparation, a *tikkùn*.

Perhaps no one grasped the distinction between memory and remembrance better than Walter Benjamin. He translated the Hebrew *zèkher* with the German *Eingedenken*, i.e. thinking-in-one (*Ein-*) with the vanquished, remembering in the unison of a word that is restored to them. The secret meeting between generations takes place in this restitution. The liberating power of remembrance does not only concern the future, but also the past.[53]

Even simply because the re-evocation of remembrance is entrusted to the word – which is neither subjective nor objective, but shared and unifying – it is not the same thing as preserving the events of the past in memory, ossified in objective form. Rather, it is to re-articulate these events, just as the word is re-articulated upon each occurrence – and thus to bring them into the present. This is indispensable in a political reading that denounces the alarming emergency of the present. Reading, at the foundations of the present, the traces of a past which is in danger of being forgotten or repressed, if not erased, is to redeem it in remembrance by elevating it to a dignified historical standing.

Yet outright oblivion is not the only danger that threatens the past. There is also a form of historical transmission, the 'history of the victors', which can be even more 'catastrophic'. For this history condemns the past to disappearance, covers it with a cumulative memory, hides it in the continuity of a reading that pretends to be objective, which seeks to impose itself as the mythology of the victors, to erase all traces of the vanquished. This is the memory of the bad conscience that seeks only to forget.

Remembrance must fight against oblivion, not for the sake of remembrance itself – which would lead to its reification – but, as per the Jewish tradition, for the sake of justice. That is why history is not an irreversible process; the struggle is open and the outcome uncertain. The history of the victors looms over us. And if the victors continue to win, '*even the dead* will not be safe'.[54] For the dead will lose any possibility of still having a voice, and nothing will be left of their name.

Fleeing the Nazis across the Pyrenees, before he turned to suicide rather than fall into their hands, Benjamin dedicated his last dramatic pages to the 'history of the vanquished', to the 'memory of the nameless'. This was both a testimony and a testament, but also already a plea, for all the Jews who would find no way out of the prison that Hitler's Europe had turned into. The history of those who were condemned to annihilation, to the obliteration even of their names, was the history of the vanquished. It would be hard to reconstruct, amidst the tears that had ripped through the fabric of history; its telling would be complex and its defence an arduous task. The Nazis would themselves threaten this history, also through the swindle that usurps the victims' place by passing them off as the victors.

Thus, Benjamin already answered one of the objections that the critics of memory would later raise against the history of the vanquished. What distinguishes their history from the victors' own? When their history is told and commemorated, does it not also transform into a victorious epic – that of the Jewish people that survived Hitler? Is it just that this people, unlike others, has on its side the injunction of memory, the obligation to tell its own story? And does this narration not itself risk being overwhelmed by conformism, becoming an object of worship, its celebration falling into the apologetic temptation?

Benjamin's response is that the history of the victims is radically different from that of the victors. It is not linear; it is made up of ruptures and intermittences. It entertains a different relationship with the past – and thus also with the future. For only the memory of the vanquished is dedicated to forgetting nothing: neither the reign of the executioners – of which it is the victim – nor the tradition of the victims, whose story it has the task of telling. It takes on the responsibility for what remains unreadable; it thus needs to be recounted again and again, so that it will not sink into the abyss. It bears the weight of the unforgettable.

10 The Future of a Negation

The 'future of a negation' is a formula coined in the French context, which has had echoes around the world. It refers to that further pathway which, having already led from annihilation to denial, finally translates into the rejection of Israel. It can be summarized as follows: since the gas chambers did not exist, and therefore the extermination of the Jews is a 'myth', nor are there any grounds for the state of Israel's existence.[55]

This same path is also taken, more or less explicitly, by those who, in addition to minimizing or normalizing the Shoah, making it a genocide like any other, see in the 'unwarranted' founding of the state of Israel the profit which the Jews cunningly took once they had entered the stage of history as victims. The more visceral the rejection of Israel, the more drastic the denial and the more strongly the idea of a conspiracy emerges. The boundaries are fluid, proving that the minimizer can slip into denialism. The rejection of Israel is, indeed, the indicator of a denial that proceeds retroactively. This is precisely where the potential force of denialism lurks today – and in this sense, far from being a marginal phenomenon, it remains the most dangerous version of conspiracy theorizing.

The seemingly harmless accusation that joins Marxists like Alain Badiou and liberals like Tzvetan Todorov in chorus is the 'sacralization of memory' that Jews have allegedly carried out over recent years and decades to justify Israel's policy of conquest.[56] This is not only the reproach aimed at the 'Holocaust industry', as it is called in the book for which Norman Finkelstein bears the sad responsibility.[57] The Jews are said to have forgotten history, to have moved from the role of victims to that of aggressors. Todorov explains, 'It is after all the basic structure of revenge – hurt suffered justifies hitting back.'[58] The first consequence of this alternative is, it would appear, the inability of Jews to have a narrative that does not turn them into either victims or heroes.

But where does this alternative come from? Who is imposing it? This question first and foremost concerns the West and Israel. For Jews, 'Never again!' had been words of redemption, of recovered dignity, faced with others and themselves. Yet, if it ever seemed certain that the memory of the unforgettable had permeated consciences, this certainty has been eroded. As commemorations spread, as museums were opened amidst great pomp and ceremony, the propensity to stigmatize Jews grew stronger. This is no paradox. The sense of guilt has been consigned to inert monuments, at the same time as it has been possible to exclude the Jewish people again, while claiming to respect morality and without too many scruples. One form of this exclusion is putting their memory on trial. The unthinkable – that their redemption would be forbidden – has increasingly become the reality. The more the West has sacralized the Holocaust, and the Jews as victims, the more abominable Israel has become, and the greater the condemnations of the 'inhumanity' said to characterize its policy.

It is worth making one thing clear, in this regard. Whatever one may think of Israeli policy, criticism is only acceptable when it separates the condemned act from the essence of the perpetrator. Because often, in the criticism directed against Israel, this essence seems to be called into question – as is Israel's very existence – together with the act being stigmatized.

Even after the Shoah, the Jews would make the bitter discovery that they were recognized only in the role of victims, in which they unwillingly found themselves. This ephemeral and fleeting recognition proceeded through a feeling of guilt – but, like all feelings, guilt comes and goes. Condemned to morbid preservation in museums, Jews have no right to exist except on account of the suffering they endured. It is as if Jews' dignity lay in their having lost the dignity that was trampled upon in the death camps, as if Jews' legitimacy could only derive from being victims, as if identity could only be *ex negativo*, in the negation of identity. The only Jew recognized is the anonymous victim and not the Jew who is in the victim. The West celebrates the destroyed, annihilated and nullified people, at the very moment that it ignores the living one. When the victim population tries to stop being a victim, to be recognized in its existence, in the possibility of a future, it meets with a sharp rejection that crystallizes in the delegitimization of the state of Israel.

Recognized only as outcasts, the Jews believed they could attain a new dignity as a people finally welcomed into the concert of nations. But they deluded themselves. The victims had the immodesty of living too long and breaking out of the condition of martyrs. They had the stubbornness to remain, to persist in their being, having resisted annihilation – to lean into an existence that can only appear obscene and aggressive in its excessive concreteness. Survival is itself almost an insult to the victim condition. And what happens if the way out of that condition translates into a political project? This is precisely what is being contested: that the Jewish people may, like others, struggle to live and have a legitimate place in history.

From this refusal stems the impossibility of getting away from the choice between victim and hero, which thus has to be endured. Those who accuse the Jewish people of exploiting memory to pursue their own interests overlook the fact that, if anything, it is the victim role that holds back the political project. And that's not to mention the contradiction in the accusation itself: on the one hand, the Jews are blamed for settling into the role of victims; on the other hand, when they try to get out of it, they are immediately branded aggressors.

In an article in *Le Monde* on 27 May 1988, the Palestinian-American intellectual Edward Said captured in a pithy phrase – cited almost as a truism – the idea that the Palestinians are the 'victim's victims'. To use an economic register, this suggests that the capital that Jews are said to draw from the Shoah is now instead transferred to the Palestinians, in whose account the very essence of victimhood is now deposited. The Jews, the victims of the Nazis, have thus become the Israeli executioners of the Palestinians. Moreover, this interpretative framework does not seem to transgress the bounds of morality, for the accusation does not exclude compassion for the original victims. Israel is recognized through an other – but only in order to get rid of Israel, which is again stripped of humanity and thus of legitimacy.[59] Precisely because the Jew was dehumanized in the extermination camps, there is a strong temptation to place Israel in the camp of the inhuman, thus freeing the West of a great sense of guilt.

Is the state of Israel not itself a concession to suffering humanity within what some have called the 'borders of

Auschwitz'?[60] This is the connection that common sense now establishes: the Shoah supposedly provides the only basis for Israel, whose existence was from the outset marked by the original sin of a foreign people that violated the right of the autochthonous and only legitimate people – the Palestinian people. The very existence of the State of Israel would then be an error, an unforeseen and unwanted return, the intrusion of the outsider, the irruption of the illegitimate, a both political and theological scandal. What is returning is in fact the ancient Israel, which ought to have been replaced by the two new monotheisms already centuries ago. The oldest of anti-Jewish themes are thus recapitulated, in a powerful crucible of denial.

The Jews' return is said to be abusive and unwarranted. But the delegitimization of their place leads to a rejection and radical denial of their right to exist. This is not a geographical question but a historical one. What is denied, when the return of the Jewish people is contested, is precisely its history – for in exile the bond with the land of Israel never faltered. History, culture, literature, ritual life and liturgical texts prove as much. And it ought to go almost without saying that Israel was already the land of *kibbutzim* and rebirth, before it had to become the land of salvation for the survivors of the death camps. Israel does not derive its justification from the Shoah, nor its identity from suffering.

As for the issue of autochthony, all peoples can be challenged to prove their right. No one is autochthonous. Rather, all are 'resident foreigners' (Leviticus 19: 33–4).[61]

11 The Singularity of the Extermination

In an interview on US television, broadcast during the United Nations General Assembly on 30 October 2009, Hugo Chávez was being pressed by a reporter about his friendship with Ahmadinejad. Seeking to get out of his obvious embarrassment, the Venezuelan leader responded with a question of his own, reproachfully asking about the genocide of the *indios* throughout the Americas. It is as if to speak of Auschwitz means being silent about the genocides, crimes and massacres committed around the rest of the world.

This attitude is much more widespread than is usually thought. It starts with a *deminutio*, questioning the figures, denouncing inflated numbers and over-dramatized events – as even authoritative figures have done. But once the minimization has begun, the door is opened to denial. Given that number was indeed in the millions, how is it even thinkable that the exact number, which will never be determined, changes the importance of the extermination conducted by the Nazis? Those who diminish and reduce want to 'demystify' the 'fable' that the Jews have been telling for decades, the extermination for which they claim a singularity said to separate it from all others. Aren't all genocides dark chapters of human history, regardless of the differences between them? Is this discussion not descending into a macabre competition?

In recent years, Jews have been pushed onto the defensive by their interlocutors, urged to talk also about the other genocides. They are called to order. Maybe it's that the death of others doesn't concern them? Perhaps it's that there are inferior, less significant dead people? Is it that the life of the German child cut short by Allied bombing in Dresden is worth less than that of the Jewish child deported to Treblinka? What about the children killed in the massacres that came before and after, from the Armenians in 1915 to the Tutsis in Rwanda in 1994? Victims are victims, always and everywhere. And genocides are always and everywhere genocides. Why, then, separate out the extermination of the Jews, distinguishing it from the others? The aporia brings into question the singularity of the Shoah.

The term 'genocide' was coined in 1944 by the jurist Raphael Lemkin, a Polish Jew who had emigrated to the United States. In December 1948, precisely because of Auschwitz, the term was adopted by the UN in a wide-ranging resolution aimed at defining all the acts which the Nuremberg tribunal had inserted within the new category 'crimes against humanity'. Paradoxically, however, this term ended up backfiring on the extermination of the Jewish people. Indeed, it seems that the underlying Jewishness of the extermination represents a threat. The issue is complex, given its many implications and connections – not least with denial. All the more regrettable are the polemical tones taken in recent times, especially by journalistic debate.

After 1945, and up till the 1960s, the extermination of Europe's Jews appeared as a tragic, yet relatively marginal, event amidst the devastation that characterized World War II. While the survivors remained silent, and the executioners took advantage of the repression of memory, the European consciousness – which had certainly not changed overnight – had a hard time facing up to the abyss of the 'final solution', the 'black hole' that had torn the modern world apart, that dialectical other face of civilization. While Auschwitz remained in the background, the singularity was diminished and its specific features appeared diluted among the many crimes that had been committed.[62] At the anti-fascist demonstrations, where, with faith in progress still intact, the Liberation was celebrated as a new triumph for enlightenment, the survivors of the Shoah paraded alongside the ex-combatants enrolled in the national cause; the Jews themselves needed to feel like citizens again, now reintegrated after years of discrimination. It would thus have seemed almost offensive to assert the singularity of the crime suffered.

Only after the Eichmann trial did Auschwitz begin to emerge from the margins and become paradigmatic of the futile suffering perpetrated in the twentieth century. Memories resurfaced, testimonies multiplied and research intensified. Thus came to light the difference between the concentration camp and the extermination camp, a distinction which had initially remained blurred. The Nazi fog which had shrouded the gas chambers began to dissipate.

As attention travelled through the concentration camp universe to reach the *Vernichtungslager*, the place of annihilation, the field of ashes, where modern consciousness took literally the replacement theology that judged the Jews to be nothing but spiritless flesh, thus reducing them to nothingness; as the foul nakedness of gassing and incineration was uncovered – the question was raised of Auschwitz's place in world history. How was this possible? Does it not seem absurd, unreasonable, unacceptable? Can it be said that this horror belongs to history? In its indecent and inexplicable abomination, did it not overturn – even in negative form – human progress, the triumphal march of Reason as depicted by Hegel? The question, dominant in the 1980s, when the abyss of the annihilation had become clear, gave rise to a more ruthless denial that more easily found a footing: the gas chambers did not take place. If Auschwitz is a 'lie', the question of its place in history does not even arise.

Those who attempt to respond bump up against an alternative whose opposing poles lead – albeit inadvertently, and by circuitous paths – to nothingness. On the one hand, there are those who claim the 'uniqueness' of Auschwitz, and make it almost a non-event – one beyond all comparison, which is placed outside of history, outside of language, and, assuming a sacral aura, can be idolized, worshipped in a silence that crosses into nothingness. On the other hand, there are those who make Auschwitz an example, however extreme, of genocide, a universal that has always marked human history in its ruthlessness. The Jew, brought back to the universalism of modernity, is said to have been annihilated in the camps just like so many other victims. Comparisons are made. And there is silence on what makes the Shoah peculiar. In the universal vacuum, its own significance is diminished. Each of these paths leads down a risky incline – and opens up room for the deniers.

What, then, is the peculiarity of the Shoah? To answer this question, Auschwitz must be reinserted into human history and, even before that, into Jewish history, with its succession of persecution, violence and oppression – with the destruction of the Second Temple under the Roman Empire, the massacres and burnings in the Spain of the marranos, right up to the pogroms that came only just before the camps. And it would be possible to recall many other exterminations in the history of Israel, of which Auschwitz is a part.

The entire history of mankind is littered with violence and massacres. What is there to be surprised about? Perhaps one should join the chorus of fatalists, according to whom there have always been genocides and there probably always will be. Was the Shoah not followed by Hiroshima and Nagasaki? And so, too, by the Vietnam War; the extermination in Cambodia; the *desaparecidos* in Argentina; the 3 million dead in the secession of Bangladesh; the massacre at Srebrenica; the slaughter in Darfur; the countless pre-emptive, unjust, forgotten wars of recent decades – all of them, without distinction, appalling.

If one takes away from the Shoah that absolute uniqueness which risks indulging Hitler's intention of beginning a new epoch in world history with the Third Reich – if one starts out from the historical event then one must be prepared to compare, that is, to establish similarities and differences. This does not mean – it is worth specifying – relativizing it. Here, a fine line has to be drawn. To consider Auschwitz one case among many, pointing only to the similarities, is to normalize it, reduce it, belittle it, as the alleged revisionists would like. Quantifying atrocities is repugnant enough already; to use one to minimize another is to wield it as a poisonous rejoinder, with the sole purpose of erasing the singularity of Auschwitz.

Although human life has the same value, the processes that lead to death are different – and the deaths themselves are different. The gas chambers, as an instrument of death, are phenomenologically, historically, politically the hallmark of the annihilation of the Jews of Europe. The gas thus has a symbolic value that must not be overlooked

– and that explains why deniers so doggedly deny the gas chambers. This is the only way to normalize Auschwitz, to make it a genocide like any other.

What then of the gulag? Perhaps the destruction of the kulaks in Stalin's Russia was less ferocious? Why only talk about Auschwitz and not about Kolyma? Are not Nazism and Stalinism the two faces of the totalitarianism that left an indelible mark on the twentieth century? This comparison, which the so-called historians' dispute in Germany revolved around, might appear antiquated and outdated, were it not for the fact that it is constantly being revived anew. Not only by deniers, for whom this is one of the best niches that they have worked their way into. But also by those who are prepared to diminish the Nazi extermination camps in order to magnify the gulag. Confusion is often sown deliberately. One embarrassing example is Tzvetan Todorov's book *Hope and Memory: Lessons from the Twentieth Century*, which, over the course of dozens and hundreds of pages, does no more than repeat one and the same thesis: that Auschwitz and Kolyma are equivalents.[63]

This equivalence has been fuelled by an idea of totalitarianism which was already widespread in the Federal Republic of Germany and has further consolidated after the fall of the Berlin Wall in 1989, with the purpose of casting a veil of silence over Nazi crimes, absolving Germany of its guilt, rehabilitating its past, and instead pointing the finger at the Stalinist terror. In its most conformist sense, totalitarianism has become the stigma with which to brand all the violence of the past century, without distinction. Totalitarianism then appears to be the ideology of modern tyranny, which, represented by Hitler, Mussolini and Stalin, was defeated by liberalism, thanks to which the West was able to resume the path of progress. The condemnation of totalitarianism is thus accompanied by the apologia of the Western order, seen as the best of possible worlds.

The comparison between Stalinism and Nazism is questionable for several reasons. Who could dispute the violence that dominated the Soviet Union for decades? The suppression of democracy and individual freedoms? The introduction of single-party rule and the state monopoly? The analogies with Nazism are obvious. However, there are also profound differences. First of all, one cannot reduce communism to Stalinism. The corruption of a project is not the project itself. The humanistic ideal of emancipation surely can be criticized, but it is not even remotely comparable to Nazism, which was the project of a perversion and, as such, from the beginning had as its goal the annihilation of the Jewish people.

Even apart from the asymmetry between their projects, the modes and results of the violence are also beyond comparison. This point is decisive. Without grasping the difference between the gulag and Auschwitz, between the labour camp and the extermination camp, it is impossible to understand the Shoah. This is not a difference of degree; it is a qualitative difference. Even Hannah Arendt perhaps contributed to obfuscating this; for although, in her work *The Origins of Totalitarianism*, she was among the first to reflect on the 'factories of death', when she mounted a comparison with the Soviet camps, she saw in Birkenau or Treblinka only an aggravated variant of the concentration camp system.[64] The labour camp and the extermination camp are both universes of death – but death plays an entirely different role in the two cases. The labour camp system, which has precursors and epigones, and which shares many features with other forms of massacre – from deportation to the branding of victims and their degradation – is encapsulated in the forced, slave-like exploitation of labour with a view to specific goals. The deportees in the Soviet Union – not only meaning the kulaks – were employed to clear entire regions of woodland, build railways and power lines, and construct urban areas. The Soviet camps were real 'industrial behemoths' that aimed to modernize the country. The cornerstone of the camp was labour; death was the ultimate consequence. In other words, the – often horrible – deaths in the labour camps were a foreseeable accident, but not a deliberately organized one.

This explains why the death rate in the gulags never exceeded 20 per cent. In Germany, the concentration camp system also consisted of labour camps, such as Buchenwald. The mortality rate there was, on average, 30 per cent. The death camps were designed for the extermination of Jews (and to some extent Roma and Sinti people). They included, in addition to Auschwitz – which was both a labour and extermination camp – Chełmno, Bełżec, Majdanek, Sobibór and Treblinka. There, the mortality rate exceeded 99 per cent; the majority of survivors came back from Auschwitz.

In the death camps, the only destination was the gas chamber. Death was both the cornerstone and the immediate purpose of these camps. The inscription *Arbeit macht frei*, which became the symbol of Auschwitz, made up a mocking part of the erasure of the crime, allowing it to begin its work. Most of the Jews who passed through that entrance would never see freedom – but nor would they see work, as they were led directly from the unloading ramps to the gas and then to the ovens. Often their stay in the camp lasted only a few hours. In the *Vernichtungslager*, efficiency was judged by the rate of extermination – that is, the number of dead. The more corpses Hitler's workshops produced, the greater the praise for their yield. In the Nazi order, even when human resources were needed for the war effort, extermination always took priority. Absolute terror produced nothing because, as Wolfgang Sofsky has observed, it was a 'purposeless . . . negative praxis' – a work of destroying without leaving traces.[65] In the gulag, the deportee was inhumanly exploited to extract minerals in the name of the 'socialist cause'; in the extermination camp, the most advanced methods of science and technology were used to turn the Jew into a product: the Jew made into a mineral. Human skin for lampshades; hair for wigs, slippers and watertight joints for submarines; ash to be spread as fertilizer; gold from teeth to be made into ingots transported to bank vaults.

In the death camps, the death industry worked day and night for the 'final solution', meaning: to eliminate the Jewish people from the planet that was to be inhabited by the 'Aryan race'. As is well known, after the wave of *Gleichschaltung*, the forcible 'coordination' of society, the violence struck at all human and social categories that were not meant to be part of the Germanic *Volk* – the disabled, homosexuals, travellers – and was then extended to prisoners of war and anti-fascist deportees. But what also distinguishes the extermination of Europe's Jews from other Nazi crimes, within which it must be contextualized, is the planetary project of the biological remodelling of humanity. The gas chamber is an inerasable place in which is inscribed the design of 'purification', with the aim of a *Judenrein* world.

Yehuda Bauer has thus spoken of total genocide.[66] The extreme limit was reached when a state, through the mouth of its Führer – its supreme authority – decided that a human group should be deprived of the right to exist on earth. Many now agree on this way of reading its singularity. The number of victims could be higher and the means of destruction more technologically powerful. Yet only once – as Saul Friedländer points out – has an extermination taken place that is an end in itself.[67]

For those who look at the Shoah from a Third World perspective, it is difficult to understand the difference from colonial genocides, which, without doubt, provided a testing ground. Laying the emphasis on what distinguishes the Shoah appears to be a case of blatant Eurocentrism. This issue is highly topical. 'No one wants to absolve the Spanish conquistadors of the massacres perpetrated in the Americas', Primo Levi wrote.[68] But the difference is that the colonial genocides had an instrumental character: entire peoples were destroyed for the sake of power, territory and wealth. The Shoah lacked such an instrumental purpose.

The extermination of the Jews of Europe is without precedent – first of all, because killing had never previously taken place on an assembly line. The process of industrializing death, which took on the almost ritualistic precision of technology, found in the use of gas not a change of degree, but a qualitative one. If there had been mass shootings already with the Einsatzgruppen, the year 1941, when the first gassings were carried out in trucks in Chełmno, was a turning point in the history of extermination. Perhaps the gassing did not mean an extra degree of suffering; it is quite possible that death from starvation and disease in the overcrowded ghettos was even worse. But gassing on an industrial scale – the use of more or less perfected techniques not to produce, but to kill, or rather to make corpses – introduced the anonymity of the executioners faced with their nameless victims. Already on the *Rampen*, those who conducted the selection could be considered not killers, but saviours. The fragmentation of the responsibility made possible its dissipation – and also allowed for the 'grey zone'. The Sonderkommando was, in this sense, the most brutal of inventions. The triumph of anonymity, which was celebrated in the gas chambers, made it possible to conceal the murder even before pulverizing the corpses, and to deny the crime even before the ashes were made into a future nothingness.

Today's denial, which is an extension of yesterday's, brings out even more clearly the singularity of Auschwitz. This is not because there are no other erasures. For instance, there is the one that has officially established itself in power in Turkey, imposing a silence over the Armenian genocide in order to maintain the fiction of a unified and pure national history. But in such attempts, circumscribed to historiography, there is no real threat of a negation that is not limited to the past, but is intended to be reiterated in the future. The difference resides precisely in this reiteration – in the renewed threat of nothingness. The desecrations of cemeteries, the burnings of synagogues, the terrorist attacks and the countless assaults, all testify to this.

With regard to the most monstrous chapter of the annihilation, that of the deported children, Levinas wrote: 'the death of martyrs, death given in the ceaseless destruction of this dignity of martyrs by the executioner, destruction whose final act is fulfilled today in the posthumous contestation of this same martyrdom by the supposed "revisers of history". Pain in its pure malignity, suffering for nothing.'[69]

12 Saying Auschwitz

The extermination of the Jews was the project of annihilating the annihilation itself. No one was meant to know: neither those who planned it, nor those operating the machinery of death, nor the supreme initiator, nor even the victims, who were condemned to disappear in the smoke, leaving no trace. The secret was supposed to destroy any revelation, any hint of a word that would direct the gaze to the human face of the drowned.

The doors of the camps have not yet closed; and if they did, they would also close on the future. It is necessary, therefore, in order not to forget the unforgettable, to break the silence, to speak the unspeakable, to the ends of the universe and beyond, where – as Paul Celan wrote – 'Nobody / bears witness for the / witness.'[70] Perhaps the age of witnessing must be followed by the age of reflection, whose most pressing task is to open up about the unspeakable.

The deniers made good use of the 'uniqueness' of Auschwitz and the prohibition imposed by Adorno already in 1949, according to which, after Auschwitz, the writing of poetry – but essentially also art itself – is 'barbaric'.[71] Many felt called into question by this. Hans Magnus Enzensberger stated in 1959: 'If we want to go on living, this sentence must be overturned.'[72] And later Peter Szondi turned the argument on its head: 'if poetry is no longer possible after Auschwitz, then it will be possible because of Auschwitz'.[73] Moreover, the rebuttal of this prohibition comes from Celan's own poetry, passed through the 'bottleneck' of the camp. It stands at the gateway between annihilated speechlessness and the turning of the breath, condensed and holding itself in, until it explodes in the *Gegenwort*, in the 'counter-word' – the revolt against the 'attack' of silence.[74] To speak is to break the silence, to shatter it, in opposition to any attempt to make Auschwitz something unspeakable, unthinkable, to dissolve it into nothingness, to annihilate it yet again.

To concede that Auschwitz is unspeakable would be to admit defeat in the struggle against the deniers. For that would mean relegating it to the domain of mystery, to the occult sphere of mysticism.[75] When it rises to the category of absolute Evil, impenetrable in its metaphysical transcendence, the Shoah is abstracted from history, removed from language. And there are many who believe that evil, through its seductive power, has an all-consuming character. Here the question takes form that more or less explicitly circulates throughout common sense, politics, history, art, psychology and philosophy: how can anyone presume to understand Auschwitz?

But understanding is not the same as explaining by causal necessity, and nor is it the same as trivializing or justifying. In understanding, there is always a remainder; understanding is at the same time a non-understanding. On the other hand, entrenching oneself behind the unspeakable, the incomprehensible, entails grave dangers. It inadvertently ends up participating in the enterprise of extermination that sought not only the erasure of consciousness and the death of bodies, but the total denial of understanding. Saying Auschwitz is the imperative that must sustain the face-to-face encounter with extermination, in the place so intangible for the denier. There can be no exchange, no discussion, no common speech with those who, by denying what happened in the past, threaten to repeat it in the future.

'The current amazement that the things we are experiencing are "still" possible in the twentieth century is *not* philosophical', Benjamin wrote.[76] This is all the more true today. Auschwitz is neither unspeakable, nor a caesura, a millennial foundation in history, as Nazism would have wanted – let alone the embodiment of an evil, perhaps in need of atonement. It is no longer possible to see Auschwitz as the closed chapter of the Nazi barbarism that once exploded into civilization, the dark side of the liberal West. One both widespread and reassuring idea considers it an expression of the collapse of reason. But, in fact, Auschwitz is the hypertrophic outcome of an instrumental rationality that made technological progress the means of domination over the other, to the point of elimination. Precisely because it represents what Primo Levi called the 'black hole' at the heart of progress, it is difficult for the modern conscience to think about it, often preferring to fill this hole with monuments or to entrust it to the archives. Auschwitz is inscribed in modernity; it is part of the world in which we continue to live and of which it remains a possible horizon. To assert that it is 'unprecedented' is to strive to seek precedents in the past and to be vigilant that it does not become a precedent in the future.

The extermination of the Jews of Europe was the extreme result of a criminal Nazi policy. It is not a matter of a past which has now been surmounted; rather, it has a bond of collusion with criminal policies in the present. Intellectual Hitlerism, in all its forms, has not been defeated. This is why the Shoah must be examined, to seek out the hidden and disturbing possibilities that modernity could still hold in store.

'Before [the Nazis] set the gas chambers into motion they had carefully tested the ground and found out to their satisfaction that no country would claim these people. The point is that a condition of complete rightlessness was created before the right to live was challenged.'[77] This reflection by Hannah Arendt on Auschwitz makes its way into our own present. It is no coincidence that the deniers profit from a nationalistic policy of 'expulsions' and 'repatriations', which has a taste for branding and special statuses – which points an accusing finger at the immigrant, the illegal, the foreigner. Antisemitism is, moreover, the archetype of all internment.

The emancipation of the Jews of Europe was announced in Clermont-Tonnerre's words to the Assemblée nationale in 1789: 'everything for the Jews as individuals, nothing for the Jews as a people'. After Auschwitz, these words took on a funereal note. They point back to the catastrophic outcome of emancipation: even those Jews who set aside their Judaism and made it a private affair, in their desire to be accepted as citizens, and conformed to the Enlightenment's luminous march, ended up being struck in the dark part of their identity. They were taken, one by one, rounded up, deported, concentrated as a people. The myth of the universal met its end in the gas chambers, where the individual Jew drowned in the anonymity of the group. In the camps, the modern Jewish condition was overturned. This dispersed people of nomads ever turned towards Zion, a people of foreigners whose transversal existence disrupted the concert of European nations, was brutally reunited so that it could be annihilated. From those same ramps where it had been sent to its death in the ovens, the Jewish people was reborn, in consciousness of a human dignity that cannot be undermined by any future denial.

The Europe that showed such indifference as it breathed in the fumes from the furnaces of the 'final solution', risking its own collapse, has a further responsibility. It bears the weight of a past that must be conjugated with the future, the duty to speak out against those who try to deny – and to declare denial a crime. It must do this, to avoid letting the world slide into the abyss of nothingness.

Antisemitism in the Twenty-First Century

Antisemitism did not end with Hitler. In the post-Nazi era it has taken on new, and often implicit, ways of evading the disapproval which it faces. The extermination of the Jews in Europe, at the cost of 6 million victims, remains engraved in the collective memory. Given the impossibility of justifying the industrialized death which was carried out on such a vast scale in the annihilation camps, 21st-century antisemitism denies the Shoah, or at least minimizes its extent and significance. This argumentative strategy makes it possible to de-legitimize Israel, which has itself become a target of stigmatization. The word 'Jew' or 'Jewish' is replaced by 'Zionist' or 'cosmopolitan', while still pointing towards an imaginary 'world Jewish conspiracy'. The most conspicuous trait that the new antisemitism has inherited from its twentieth-century counterpart is its propensity for conspiracy theory. The novelty lies in the global character of Judaeophobia, which has now spread to every part of the world.[1]

Definition – The term 'antisemitism', which continues to be used to refer generically to hostility towards Jews, today appears more problematic than ever on account of the confusions to which it can lead. By 'antisemitism' in the strict sense, we mean the racist variant of Judaeophobia that prevailed in the modern era.[2]

Coined in 1860 by Moritz Steinschneider, an Austrian Jew who wanted to denounce prejudice, the adjective *antisemitisch* was taken up by the ideologue Wilhelm Marr as the banner of the Antisemiten-Liga (League of Antisemites), founded on 26 September 1879. Marr set out to distinguish his own battle, based on the pseudo-scientific theme of 'race', from the old religious hatred. Without doubt, he largely succeeded in this attempt.

This antisemitism, which some call 'modern' and others 'racist', is the source of at least two serious misunderstandings. Because of the great degree of intermixing throughout their history, Jews cannot be considered 'Semites' in the old ethnic sense of the word – all the more so since 'Semites' also include Arabs, whereas antisemitism, in this ideological-political usage, targets Jews alone. It would be more accurate to speak of anti-Jewish hatred. The second misunderstanding resides in the racist prejudice that the term conveys. Here we must warn against the danger of becoming hostages to racial mythology. In short, those who speak of 'antisemitism' end up believing, and having others believe, that Jews, as 'Semites', are a separate 'race', as opposed to 'Aryans'.

Hence the commonplace idea that antisemitism is a specific form of racism. This simplifies this phenomenon, restricting its scope to modernity and eliminating many of its constituent elements – first and foremost, the theological ones. Just as racism ought to have died out, so, too, should antisemitism, with the end of the Nazi regime that made it the cornerstone of its ideology, be a mere residue on the path to extinction. Yet this optimistic conjecture is not borne out by the reality of either case.

Many scholars in the post-war period already lamented the uncritical use of a bad term. The term 'antisemitism' extends far beyond the category of racism, thus adding to its ambiguity. Forms of anti-Jewish violence, such as those intended to strike at 'Zionists', claim to draw on anti-racist positions. Precisely to avoid misunderstandings, the European Monitoring Centre on Racism and Xenophobia (EUMC) issued a document in 2005 in which it reiterated that antisemitism can also 'target the state of Israel, conceived as a Jewish community'.

The continuity of Jew-hate – Antisemitism is a complex and heterogeneous phenomenon, and it has not remained unchanged. There is no eternal antisemitism that always has the same causes and modalities.[3] Although Jew-hate seems to be the most enduring and intense form, it nevertheless remains connected to history and linked both to the different situations of the Jewish people who have suffered its violence, and to the ideologies that fuelled it.[4] New stigmas overlap with the ones that went before, and forgotten accusations resurface with unprecedented emphases.

For proof of this, we need only look to the distinction between two great epochs: on the one hand, the ancient one inspired by religious anti-Judaism, and on the other, the modern, secular one dominated by racist theories. Today, a third is added – that of the new Judaeophobia which, having been latent after World War II, exploded in full force on the verge of the new millennium.[5] The connection between these three eras is highly controversial. The last one, however, has helped to shed light on the continuity between the first two, revealing the theological matrix of many political stigmas.[6]

The 'Jewish question' before and after the Shoah – In Christian eschatology, Jews must be preserved for conversion on the Day of Judgement. In the secularized apocalypse of modernity, the Jew is no longer a necessary witness and can be eliminated. Antisemitism gains in intensity because, starting with blood, invariable characteristics are attributed to 'the Jew', considered in his supposedly unsalvageable essence.

In the Age of Enlightenment, when equality is granted and emancipation is supposedly achieved, the so-called 'Jewish question' – as Hannah Arendt emphasized – is raised by the non-Jewish world because Judaism seems to be a question mark, a problem to be solved.[7] It is not just a religion, like Christianity. If that were the case, freedom of religion would be the solution. But the Jews are also a people. The secular Jew does not thereby cease to be a Jew. And if that is the case, then the question is not so much religious as political: Jews are unassimilable foreigners who embody the threat of a 'state within a state'. One can guess why the 'invisible Jew' – that is, the emancipated Jew no longer recognizable in the public space – becomes an obsession.

There remains the traditional repertoire of anti-Jewish myths, which amount to just as many accusations: deicide, their cursed wandering, hatred of humanity, ritual murder, a chosenness seen as racism, perfidy and usury, and conspiracy.[8] But everything is reinterpreted in the light of the 'lie', the accusation that has pervaded modernity for centuries and culminated in Hitler's *Mein Kampf*: Jews falsify and lie, they pass themselves off as Germans, as French, etc., while they are in fact 'foreigners'; they make people believe they are something that they are not and hide their constitutive nothingness.[9] Thus, three stages are set out: stigmatization, segregation, annihilation.[10]

After the Shoah, whenever it is denied that the extermination took place, the Jew continues to be seen as the foreigner who corrodes, pollutes, poisons, with the politico-cosmic strategy of achieving world domination.

Conspiracy theorizing – The accusation that Jews spin together plots, primarily for the sake of establishing their own domination, has been repeated since antiquity. Yet it has taken on a decisive role in recent decades. Even when it comes to the myth of the 'Jewish plot', the political categories translate an apocalyptic religious substratum, in which the Jew is the embodiment of the antichrist. Antisemitic mobilization draws on the symbolic archive of Christian anti-Judaism to imprint its secular version with the aura of mystery and elevate the Jew to an eschatological enemy.

Especially vilified is the chosenness of the Jewish people, denounced as a sign of intolerable arrogance. To this is added the idea that the Jews possess a secret that constitutes their mythical, arcane power, able to open the way to world domination.

The history of this myth follows a crescendo: the local conspiracy in the Middle Ages (think of the Jewish-leprous conspiracy that so agitated the entire fourteenth century, with the poisoning of the wells), the national conspiracy in modern times (for instance, the Dreyfus affair in France between 1894 and 1906), the international conspiracy at the beginning of the twentieth century, and finally the global conspiracy of recent decades.

Globalization fuels and strengthens the myth of the Jewish conspiracy which breaks away from any local basis. Not so much the diaspora of old, but rather the new uprooting process caused by emancipation, trade, the cult of money, and democratic individualism, is said to be the condition whereby the Jews – those foreigners who cannot be assimilated within nations, maintaining ties of solidarity among themselves – can spin a web around the globe, a plot of universal Jewish domination that extends around the planet.

While there is no lack of important precedents, it was the publication of the *Protocols of the Elders of Zion*, a forgery fabricated in Paris in the early twentieth century, that marked a watershed in the history of the conspiracy.[11] In the fictitious figures of the 'Elders of Zion' converge the ancient sages of Israel, who from the time of Solomon are said to have hatched a plot against mankind; the Zionist leaders, starting with Theodor Herzl; and the unknown puppet-masters who are said to have pulled the strings of the plot. It is no coincidence that the dissemination of the *Protocols* coincided with Zionist congresses: the first in 1897, and the sixth in 1903.

But the so-called 'Jewish danger', above all, meant Jewish Bolshevism – the proof of the power that the Jewish intelligentsia had already gained, thanks to the October Revolution. The Nazi ideologues used the *Protocols* to substantiate the thesis of the Jewish menace that had taken form in Bolshevism.[12]

To believe conspiracy theories is to accept a summary and magical view of history in which everything can be traced back to a single cause acting with subjective will. The more complex the scenario, the greater the anxiety to find a culprit. There is no event – unemployment, war, poverty, migratory movements – that does not have its imaginary scapegoat. The conspiracy has thus become a recurring propaganda topos. Since the beginning of the new century, marked by 11 September, it is possible to speak of the hegemony of conspiratorial thinking, which feeds on fake news thanks to the Internet. Defined on each occasion by their alleged goals – domination, dispossession, 'ethnic replacement' – the Jew is once again the absolute enemy.

But, more than the individual Jew, it is Israel that is targeted. It is considered – far beyond the state itself – the organizational powerhouse that undermines the world's balance and holds the reins of the global plot.

Anti-Zionism – Since the 1960s, Judaeophobia has entered a new phase, by taking the particular form of anti-Zionism.

Deemed a form of racism, Zionism was condemned by Resolution 3379 adopted by the UN General Assembly on 10 November 1975. Although it was repealed in 1991, this Resolution contributed to the hostility towards Israel, which reached its peak at the world conference held in Durban from 31 August to 8 September 2001. Already during the preparatory phase of the UN Conference for the countries of the Asian region, which took place in Tehran, the Arab states assumed a growing hegemony and eventually pushed through a text in which, while the state of Israel was accused of ethnic cleansing, Zionism was referred to as a 'new form of apartheid', based on 'racial superiority'. Despite the voices raised against this demonization, the idea that Zionism is not only a nationalism, but also a colonialism, an imperialism, an apartheid regime, remains deep-rooted.

Everything that can no longer be said openly against the Jews is said against Israel, a name that, in the ambiguity of its meaning, is used to denote both the state of Israel and biblical Israel – that is, the Jewish people. As has been said many times, this is not a matter of criticism of Israeli government policy, but of speech that delegitimizes Israel. Thus, every Jew living in the diaspora, despite not being an Israeli citizen and not taking part in Israeli elections, is forced to answer for the policy of a government which she has not chosen. Hence the synonymy of 'Jew' and 'Zionist'. In this totalizing move, which lays blame on the individual *because they are Jewish*, should be seen the same mechanism that led to the extermination.

At the basis of anti-Zionism, it is not difficult to recognize ancient prejudices as well as more recent rhetorical strategies. The old accusation of 'racism' re-emerges – or, better, becomes a prominent feature of anti-Zionist propaganda. Most striking is the Nazification of the Jews that makes Israel a state assimilated to the Third Reich. The swapping of roles was begun by Edward Said who, writing in *Le Monde* on 27 May 1988, endorsed the idea that the Jews, victims of the Nazis, had become the Israeli executioners of the Palestinians. With this moral flippancy, the West can rid itself of its cumbersome guilt by once again depriving Israel of humanity.

As the commemorations became more widespread, the propensity to stigmatize and excoriate Jews grew stronger. The idea took hold that the state of Israel was granted to the victims within the 'borders of Auschwitz'.[13] In this view, the Shoah alone provided a foundation for Israel, whose existence is marked from the very beginning by the 'original sin' of having violated, as a foreign and occupying people, the right of the only 'autochthonous' people, the only legitimate one – meaning the Palestinian people. Israel challenges the sovereign self-consciousness of nations by reminding them that no one is autochthonous.[14] To dispute the return of the Jews, however, is also to deny the history of this people, which in twenty centuries of exile, along the narrative thread that weaves its identity, has never severed its bond with *Eretz Israel*, with the land of Israel. This is testified by literature, liturgical texts, and the remembrance nourished in daily life. Nor can it be overlooked that Israel was already the land of the *kibbutzim* long before it became the haven for survivors.

However, today we can speak of a tragic trait of Zionism that the official epic ignores. On the threshold of the twentieth century, Theodor Herzl believed he was solving the 'Jewish question' by asserting the Jews' claim to a state and citizenship, the two pillars of modernity. Normalization came through a reduction of the people to the nation. But if, before, the individual Jew was an outsider, now the state of Israel is the pariah among nations.

Geopolitical issues have a theological substratum. The return of Israel, the unexpected rebirth of Jewish Jerusalem after the Six Day War in 1967, was a scandal for the other two monotheisms, which had imagined that its history was over already. This is especially true of Islam, which could only admit the presence of the Jewish people as *dhimmi* – as its subjects.

In recent decades, the Jewish people has been increasingly desemiticized, de-historicized, to the point of becoming emblematic of the West. There has been a strong Islamization of Judaeophobia, which can turn from the denial of Israel's right to exist to the desire to destroy it. Jew-hate has a history in radical Islamism, intertwined with Nazism's own history through the figure of the Grand Mufti of Jerusalem, Haj Amin al-Husseini. But the role of ideologues like Sayyid Qutb cannot be underestimated, either. Global jihad, in its different versions – from the Iranian version to those of Al-Qaeda, Hamas, Hezbollah and finally ISIS – points to the Jews as the worldwide enemies that must be eliminated everywhere – as illustrated by the various attacks also in European countries.[15] In a cosmic and Manichaean vision, here, too, emerges the image of a people that is both a visible vanguard and an occult power that manipulates and steers the world's fate.

Denialism – Conspiratorial ideology, pervaded by hatred and combined with the myth of the Jew as master of deception, has given rise to the phenomenon of denialism, which has been able to spread in recent years also thanks to the new media. Originating in 1948 in France with the publications of Paul Rassinier, it was revived in the 1970s by Robert Faurisson, who helped to disseminate it overseas. One of its leading exponents was David Irving, who, as we have seen, in 2000 brought the historian Deborah Lipstadt to court in a libel case. She then authored the book *History on Trial: My Day in Court with a Holocaust Denier*, which was made into a film. Roger Garaudy's 1995 pamphlet *The Founding Myths of Modern Israel* opened a new chapter of anti-Zionist denialism.

Denial brings together different fronts, from the new Hitlerites to Islamic fundamentalists. It can also have an official, or even outright governmental, guise, as in the emblematic case of Ahmadinejad's Iran, which denied the Shoah in the UN General Assembly on 23 September 2011.

It would be a mistake to reduce denialism to a matter of historiographical debate. The famous historian Pierre Vidal-Naquet called deniers 'the assassins of memory'. But the expression is reductive, because denialism does not only concern the past, but the future, too. Denialism presents itself as the denunciation of a 'lie'. The German neo-Nazi Thies Christophersen called his 1973 book *Die Auschwitz-Lüge*. In short: the gas chambers never existed, the extermination never took place, the Shoah is a 'fable' that the Jews spin, an imposture from which they want to profit. The first outcome of this 'scam' is said to be the state of Israel, whose existence is thereby delegitimized.

The allegation that a plot is afoot is the cornerstone of denialism. While it boasts of its novelty in dismantling myths, it is as old as antisemitism itself.

Notes

The New Denialism

1 Primo Levi, *The Drowned and the Saved*, New York: Simon & Schuster, 2017, p. 1.
2 See Jean-François Lyotard, *Le différend*, Paris: Les Éditions de Minuit, 1983, pp. 16ff.
3 Paul Celan, 'Ashglory' in *Breathturn,* Los Angeles: Sun & Moon Press, 1995, p. 179.
4 See Shlomo Venezia, *Inside the Gas Chambers: Eight Months in the Sonderkommando of Auschwitz*, Cambridge: Polity, 2009. Shlomo Venezia's book was first published in French with a preface by Simone Veil, also in 2007.
5 Henry Rousso, 'La négation du génocide juif', *L'Histoire*, 106, 1987, pp. 76–9.
6 Raul Hilberg, *The Destruction of the European Jews*, New Haven: Yale University Press, 2003.
7 See Jean-Claude Milner, *Les penchants criminels de l'Europe démocratique*, Paris: Verdier, 2003, pp. 68ff.
8 There has been a stir over the many cases of high school teachers and university professors whose actions would be difficult to explain within this neo-Enlightenment perspective.
9 Wellers returned to the subject two years later. See *Les chambres à gaz ont existé: des documents, des témoignages, des chiffres*, Paris: Gallimard, 1981.

10 Valérie Igounet, *Le négationnisme en France*, Paris: Que sais-je?, 2020, p. 6.
11 Pierre Vidal-Naquet, *Assassins of Memory: Essays on the Denial of the Holocaust*, New York: Columbia University Press, 1993. See the interview 'Le Pen: ma philosophie', granted by Jean-Marie Le Pen to *National-Hebdo*, 98, 1986, p. 6.
12 Pierre-André Taguieff, *L'imaginaire du complot mondial: aspects d'un mythe moderne*, Paris: Éditions Mille et une nuits, 2006, p. 24.
13 A phrase of Roger Garaudy's. See section 5, 'In the Shallows of Denial', in 'If Auschwitz Is Nothing', below.
14 On the question of 'uniqueness', see section 11, 'The Singularity of the Extermination', in 'If Auschwitz Is Nothing', below.
15 [Translator's note: A reference to the Italian neofascist group CasaPound, which describes itself in these terms.]
16 Here it is worth mentioning the explicit reference to conspiracy in the working definition of Holocaust denial provided by the International Holocaust Remembrance Alliance: 'Holocaust denial in its various forms is an expression of antisemitism. The attempt to deny the genocide of the Jews is an effort to exonerate National Socialism and antisemitism from guilt or responsibility in the genocide of the Jewish people. Forms of Holocaust denial also include blaming the Jews for either exaggerating or creating the Shoah for political or financial gain as if the Shoah itself was the result of a conspiracy plotted by the Jews. In this, the goal is to make the Jews culpable and antisemitism once again legitimate.' See www.holocaustremembrance.com/resources/working-definitions-charters/working-definition-holocaust-denial-and-distortion.
17 See Donatella Di Cesare, *Il complotto al potere*, Turin: Einaudi, 2021, pp. 78ff.

If Auschwitz Is Nothing

1 Heinrich Himmler's Posen speech, 4 October 1943, text from jewishvirtuallibrary.org.
2 Jacques Derrida, *Cinders*, Lincoln: University of Nebraska Press, 1991, p. 57.
3 Ibid., p. 59.
4 Pierre Vidal-Naquet himself explains: 'I have borrowed the term, with his permission, from Yosef Yerushalmi . . . [he] used it with reference to the "revisionists" on June 3, 1987, during a colloquium on forgetting': see *Assassins of Memory: Essays on*

the Denial of the Holocaust, New York: Columbia University Press, 1993, p. 146.

5 Raul Hilberg, *The Destruction of the European Jews*, New Haven: Yale University Press, 2003, pp. 51ff.

6 Emmanuel Levinas, 'Reflections on the Philosophy of Hitlerism', *Critical Inquiry*, 17, 1, Autumn 1990, pp. 62–71.

7 Ibid., p. 64.

8 Ibid., p. 69.

9 Ibid.

10 Ibid., p. 71.

11 Götz Aly, *Aktion T4: die Euthanasie-Zentrale in der Tiergartenstrasse 4*, Berlin: Hentrich, 1989.

12 Philippe Burrin, *Nazi Anti-Semitism: From Prejudice to the Holocaust*, New York: The New Press, 2005.

13 Léon Poliakov, *The Aryan Myth: A History of Racist and Nationalist Ideas in Europe*, New York: Barnes & Noble Books, 1996.

14 Adolf Hitler, *Mein Kampf*, London: Houghton Mifflin Company, 1939, pp. 238ff. The first volume of *Mein Kampf* dates to 1925, and the second to 1926. For a more in-depth discussion of this theme, I refer the reader to Donatella Di Cesare 'Lies and Fakery: The Non-Being of the Jew in *Mein Kampf*', pp. 59ff. in Di Cesare, *Heidegger and the Jews: The Black Notebooks*, Cambridge: Polity, 2018.

15 Hitler, *Mein Kampf*, p. 244.

16 Ibid.

17 Victor Klemperer, *The Language of the Third Reich: LTI – Lingua Tertii Imperii*, London: Bloomsbury, 2013, p. 29.

18 Ibid.

19 See Giorgio Agamben, 'State of Exception', in *The Omnibus* Homo Sacer, Stanford University Press, 2017 (II, i).

20 Primo Levi, *Opere,* ed. Marco Belpoliti, Vol. II, Turin: Einaudi, 2017, pp. 1012–13.

21 'Protocol of the Wannsee Conference, January 20, 1942', text from yadvashem.org.

22 Nadine Fresco, 'Les redresseurs de morts', *Les Temps Modernes*, 1980, pp. 2150–2211. See also her *Fabrication d'un antisémite*, Paris: Seuil, 1999.

23 [Translator's note: The pamphlet was published in English as *Crossing the Line.*]

24 See Vidal-Naquet, *Assassins of Memory*, pp. 17, 69–70.

25 Michael Shermer and Alex Grobman, *Denying History: Who Says the Holocaust Never Happened and Why Do They Say It?*, Berkeley: University of California Press, 2009.

26 Deborah Lipstadt, *History on Trial: My Day in Court with a Holocaust Denier*, New York: HarperPerennial, 2008.
27 The main denialist sites are: the Zündelsite; Greg Raven and Fred Leuchter's pages; the Committee for Open Debate on the Holocaust, headed by Bradley Smith, responsible for the spread of denialism in US universities; and the Association des Anciens Amateurs de Récits de Guerres et d'Holocaustes (AAARGH) belonging to the Adelaide Institute, which tries to adopt a neutral tone in order to pass itself off as a centre for historical documentation. One bulwark against all this is the Israeli site Nizkor – Hebrew for 'we will remember' – www.nizkor.org; since 1992 it has taken on the dual task of both monitoring and denouncing denialist sites, and providing precise counter-information.
28 Out of the over 500,000 Jews who had lived in that country in 1933, only 3,000 remained by 1945.
29 See *Historikerstreit. Die Dokumentation der Kontroverse um die Einzigartigkeit der nationalsozialistischen Judenvernichtung*, Munich/Zurich: Piper, 1987.
30 Ernst Nolte, *Der europäische Bürgerkrieg 1917–1945: Nationalsozialismus und Bolschewismus*, Munich: Herbig, 2000.
31 This 'normalization' of the past was aided by Habermas's insipid response: while condemning the revisionists' 'apologetic tendencies', he provided his own support for national identity, based on a 'constitutional patriotism'.
32 As in the title of Klaus-Michael Mallmann and Martin Cüppers's *Halbmond und Hakenkreuz: Das Dritte Reich, die Araber und Palästina*, Darmstadt: Primus Verlag, 2014.
33 Jeffrey Herf, *Nazi Propaganda for the Arab World*, New Haven: Yale University Press, 2011.
34 'Some Elementary Comments on the Rights of Freedom of Expression', text from chomsky.info.
35 See Robert Faurisson, *Mémoire en defense contre ceux qui m'accusent de falsifier l'histoire: la questione des chambres à gaz*, Paris: La Vieille Taupe, Paris 1980. See also Valérie Igounet, *Robert Faurisson: portrait d'un négationniste*, Paris: Denoêl, 2012.
36 See Pierre Vidal-Naquet, 'On Faurisson and Chomsky', in *Assassins of Memory*.
37 Robert Faurisson, 'Je cherche midi à midi', *Les Nouvelles Littéraires*, 1977, pp. 10–17.
38 Primo Levi, *If This Is a Man*, New York: The Orion Press, 1959, p. 24.

39 On this, see Till Bastian, *Auschwitz und die 'Auschwitz-Lüge': Massenmord, Geschichtsfälschung und die deutsche Identität*, Bonn: Bundeszentrale für politische Bildung, 2016.
40 Henry Rousso, *Le syndrome de Vichy de 1944 à nos jours*, Paris: Seuil, 1990, p. 163.
41 *The Leuchter Report: The First Forensic Examination of Auschwitz*, London: Focal Point Publications, 1989.
42 Georges Wellers, 'Der "Leuchter-Bericht" über die Gaskammern von Auschwitz: Revisionistische Propaganda und Leugnung der Wahrheit', *Dachauer Hefte*, 7, 1991, p. 237.
43 Werner Wegner, 'Keine Massenvergasungen in Auschwitz? Zur Kritik des Leuchter-Gutachtens', in *Die Schatten der Vergangenheit. Impulse zur Historisierung des Nationalsozialismus*, ed. Uwe Backes, Frankfurt am Main /Berlin: Propyläen, 1990, pp. 450ff.
44 Günther Anders, *Wir Eichmannsöhne: offener Brief an Klaus Eichmann*, Munich: Beck, 1964.
45 Shlomo Venezia, *Inside the Gas Chambers: Eight Months in the Sonderkommando of Auschwitz*, Cambridge: Polity, 2009, p. 54.
46 Ibid., pp. 66–73.
47 Primo Levi, *The Drowned and the Saved*, New York: Simon & Schuster, 2017, p. 21, translation edited.
48 Primo Levi, 'Prefazione' in *La vita offesa: storia e memoria dei Lager nazisti nei racconti di duecento sopravvissuti*, edited by Anna Bravo and Daniele Jalla, Milan: Franco Angeli, 1986, p. 9.
49 Paul Ricœur, *Das Rätsel der Vergangenheit. Erinnern – Vergessen – Verzeihen*, Göttingen: Wallstein, 1998; see also his *Memory, History, Forgetting*, University of Chicago Press, 2010.
50 Régine Robin, *La mémoire saturée*, Paris: Stock, 2003.
51 Peter Novick, *The Holocaust in American Life*, Boston: Houghton Mifflin Company, 1999.
52 Avishai Margalit, *The Ethics of Memory*, Cambridge, MA: Harvard University Press, 2002.
53 Walter Benjamin, 'On the Concept of History', in *Selected Writings*, Vol. IV: *1938–1940*, ed. Howard Eiland and Michael W. Jennings, Cambridge, MA: Harvard University Press, 2003.
54 Ibid.
55 This phrase was introduced by Alain Finkielkraut, *L'avenir d'une négation: réflexions sur la question du genocide*, Paris: Seuil, 1982 (in English: *The Future of a Negation: Reflections on the Question of Genocide*, Lincoln: University of Nebraska

Press, 1998). It was subsequently taken up several times, notably by Éric Marty in his polemic with Alain Badiou. See 'Alain Badiou: l'avenir d'une negation', in Marty, *Une querelle avec Alain Badiou, philosophe*, Paris: Gallimard, 2007, pp. 41–94.

56 See Alain Badiou, *Circonstances 3: portées du mot 'juif'*, Paris: Lignes, 2005; Tzvetan Todorov, *Hope and Memory: Lessons from the Twentieth Century*, Princeton University Press, 2016.

57 Norman Finkelstein, *The Holocaust Industry: Reflections on the Exploitation of Jewish Suffering*, London: Verso, 2001.

58 Todorov, *Hope and Memory*, p. 167.

59 Elhanan Yakira, *Post-sionisme, post-Shoah: trois essais sur une négation, une délégitimation et une diabolisation d'Israël*, Paris: Presses universitaires de France, 2010, pp. 256ff.

60 Shmuel Trigano, *Les frontières de Auschwitz*, Paris: Le Livre de Poche, 2005.

61 For a further discussion of these themes, I refer the reader to Donatella Di Cesare, *Israele: terra, ritorno, anarchia*, Turin: Bollati Boringhieri, 2012; and *Resident Foreigners: A Philosophy of Migration*, Cambridge: Polity, 2020.

62 See Enzo Traverso, *Auschwitz e gli intellettuali: La Shoah nella cultura del dopoguerra*, Bologna: il Mulino, pp. 227ff.

63 Todorov, *Hope and Memory*.

64 Hannah Arendt, *The Origins of Totalitarianism*, San Diego: Harcourt Brace, 1968.

65 Wolfgang Sofsky, *The Order of Terror: The Concentration Camp*, Princeton University Press, 2013, p. 21.

66 See Yehuda Bauer, *Rethinking the Holocaust*, Boulder: Colorado University Press, 2013.

67 Saul Friedländer, 'Die "Endlösung". Über das Unbehagen der Geschichtsdeutung', in *Der historische Ort des Nationalsozialismus. Annäherungen*, ed. Walter Pehle, Frankfurt: Fischer, 1990.

68 Levi, *The Drowned and the Saved*, p. 11.

69 Emmanuel Levinas, *Entre nous: essais sur le penser-à-l'autre*, Paris: Grasset, 2016.

70 Paul Celan, 'Ashglory' in *Breathturn,* Los Angeles: Sun & Moon Press, 1995, p. 179.

71 Theodor W. Adorno, 'Cultural Criticism and Society', in *Prisms*, Cambridge, MA: MIT Press, 1983, p. 34.

72 Hans Magnus Enzensberger, *Einzelheiten*, Frankfurt: Suhrkamp, 1962, p. 249.

73 Peter Szondi, *Schriften II*, Frankfurt: Suhrkamp, 1978, p. 383.

74 Paul Celan, 'Straitening', in *The Selected Poems and Prose of Paul Celan*, New York: W. W. Norton, 2002.

75 Giorgio Agamben, *Quel che resta di Auschwitz: l'archivio e il testimone*, Turin: Bollati Boringhieri, 1998, pp. 30ff.
76 Benjamin, 'On the Concept of History', p. 392.
77 Arendt, *The Origins of Totalitarianism*, p. 296.

Antisemitism in the Twenty-First Century

1 Daniel Goldhagen, *The Devil that Never Dies: The Rise and Threat of Global Antisemitism*, New York: Little Brown, 2013.
2 Shulamit Volkov, *Germans, Jews and Antisemites: Trials in Emancipation*, Cambridge University Press, 2006.
3 Walter Laqueur, *The Changing Face of Anti-Semitism: From Ancient Time to the Present Day*, Oxford University Press, 2006.
4 Robert S. Wistrich, *A Lethal Obsession: Anti-Semitism from Antiquity to the Global Jihad*, New York: Random House, 2010.
5 Pierre-André Taguieff, *Judéophobie: la dernière vague (2000–2018)*, Paris: Fayard, 2018; see also his *L'antisémitisme*, Paris: Presses universitaires de France, 2015.
6 Giovanni Miccoli, 'Racines chrétiennes et contribution catholique à l'essor de l'antisémitisme politique', in *Antisémythes: l'image des Juifs entre culture et politique (1848–1939)*, ed. Marie-Anne Matard-Bonucci, Paris: École française de Rome, 2005, pp. 43–52.
7 See Hannah Arendt, 'The Enlightenment and the Jewish Question', in *The Jewish Writings*, ed. Jerome Kohn and Ron H. Feldman, New York: Schocken Books, 2007. See also her *The Origins of Totalitarianism.*
8 See, for instance, Marcello Massenzio, *Le Juif errant ou l'art de survivre*, Paris: Cerf, 2010.
9 Adolf Hitler, *Mein Kampf*, London: Houghton Mifflin Company, 1939. The first volume of *Mein Kampf* dates to 1925, and the second to 1926.
10 See Raul Hilberg, *The Destruction of the European Jews*, New Haven: Yale University Press, 2003.
11 See Norman Cohn, *Warrant for Genocide: The Myth of the Jewish World Conspiracy and the Protocols of the Elders of Zion*, London: Serif, 2006.
12 See Paul Hanebrink, *A Specter Haunting Europe: The Myth of Judeo-Bolshevism*, Cambridge, MA: Belknap Press of Harvard University Press, 2018.
13 Trigano, *Les frontières de Auschwitz.*

14 See Donatella Di Cesare, *Israele: terra, ritorno, anarchia*, Turin: Bollati Boringhieri, 2012.
15 Jeffrey Herf, *Nazi Propaganda for the Arab World*, New Haven: Yale University Press, 2011.

Bibliography

Agamben, Giorgio, *Quel che resta di Auschwitz: l'archivio e il testimone*, Turin: Bollati Boringhieri, 1998.
Agamben, Giorgio, 'State of Exception', in *The Omnibus* Homo Sacer, Stanford University Press, 2017.
Aly, Götz, *Aktion T4: die Euthanasie-Zentrale in der Tiergartenstrasse 4*, Berlin: Hentrich, 1989.
Anders, Günther, *Wir Eichmannsöhne: offener Brief an Klaus Eichmann*, Munich: Beck, 1964.
Arendt, Hannah, *The Origins of Totalitarianism*, San Diego: Harcourt Brace, 1968.
Arendt, Hannah, 'The Enlightenment and the Jewish Question', in *The Jewish Writings*, ed. Jerome Kohn and Ron H. Feldman, New York: Schocken Books, 2007.
Augstein, Rudolf, Karl Dietrich Bracher, Martin Broszat, Jürgen Habermas et al., *Historikerstreit. Die Dokumentation der Kontroverse um die Einzigartigkeit der nationalsozialistischen Judenvernichtung*, Munich and Zurich: Piper, 1987.
Badiou, Alain, *Circonstances 3: portées du mot 'juif'*, Paris: Lignes, 2005.
Bastian, Till, *Auschwitz und die 'Auschwitz-Lüge': Massenmord, Geschichtsfälschung und die deutsche Identität*, Bonn: Bundeszentrale für politische Bildung, 2016.
Bauer, Yehuda, *Rethinking the Holocaust*, Boulder: Colorado University Press, 2013.

Benjamin, Walter, 'On the Concept of History', in *Selected Writings*, Vol. IV: *1938–1940*, ed. Howard Eiland and Michael W. Jennings, Cambridge, MA: Harvard University Press, 2003.

Bertolini, Frida, *Gli inganni della memoria: testimonianza, falsificazioni, negazioni*, Milan: Mimesis, 2016.

Burrin, Philippe, *Nazi Anti-Semitism: From Prejudice to the Holocaust*, New York: The New Press, 2005.

Celan, Paul, *Breathturn,* Los Angeles: Sun & Moon Press, 1995.

Celan, Paul, *The Selected Poems and Prose of Paul Celan*, New York: W. W. Norton, 2002.

Cohn, Norman, *Warrant for Genocide: The Myth of the Jewish World Conspiracy and the Protocols of the Elders of Zion*, London: Serif, 2006.

Derrida, Jacques *Cinders*, Lincoln: University of Nebraska Press, 1991.

Di Cesare, Donatella, *Israele: terra, ritorno, anarchia*, Turin: Bollati Boringhieri, 2012.

Di Cesare, Donatella, *Heidegger and the Jews: The Black Notebooks*, Cambridge: Polity, 2018.

Di Cesare, Donatella, *Resident Foreigners: A Philosophy of Migration*, Cambridge: Polity, 2020.

Di Cesare, Donatella, *Il complotto al potere*, Turin: Einaudi, 2021.

Finkielkraut, Alain, *The Future of a Negation: Reflections on the Question of Genocide*, Lincoln: University of Nebraska Press, 1998.

Flores, Marcello, 'Negazionismi, revisionismi e libertà d'opinone', *Il Mulino*, 3, 2007, pp. 525–36.

Flores, Marcello, *Cattiva memoria: perché è difficile fare i conti con la storia*, Bologna: il Mulino, 2020.

Fresco, Nadine, 'Les redresseurs de morts', *Les Temps Modernes*, 1980, pp. 2150–211.

Fresco, Nadine, *Fabrication d'un antisémite*, Paris: Seuil, 1999.

Friedländer, Saul, 'Die 'Endlösung'. Über das Unbehagen der Geschichtsdeutung', in *Der historische Ort des Nationalsozialismus. Annäherungen*, ed. Walter Pehle, Frankfurt: Fischer, 1990.

Friedländer, Saul, *Nazi Germany and the Jews: The Years of Persecution, 1933–1939*, New York: HarperCollins, 1997.

Friedländer, Saul, *The Years of Extermination: Nazi Germany and the Jews, 1939–1945*, New York: HarperCollins, 2007.

Goldhagen, Daniel, *The Devil that Never Dies: The Rise and Threat of Global Antisemitism*, New York: Little Brown, 2013.

Hanebrink, Paul, *A Specter Haunting Europe: The Myth of*

Judeo-Bolshevism, Cambridge, MA: Belknap Press of Harvard University Press, 2018.

Herf, Jeffrey, *Nazi Propaganda for the Arab World*, New Haven: Yale University Press, 2011.

Hilberg, Raul, *The Destruction of the European Jews*, New Haven: Yale University Press, 2003.

Igounet, Valérie, *Robert Faurisson: portrait d'un négationniste*, Paris: Denoël, 2012.

Igounet, Valérie, *Le négationnisme en France*, Paris: Que sais-je?, 2020.

Klemperer, Victor, *The Language of the Third Reich: LTI – Lingua Tertii Imperii*, London: Bloomsbury, 2013.

Laqueur, Walter, *The Terrible Secret: Suppression of the Truth About Hitler's 'Final Solution'*, Florence: Giuntina, 1983.

Laqueur, Walter, *The Changing Face of Anti-Semitism: From Ancient Time to the Present Day*, Oxford University Press, 2006.

Levi, Primo, *If This Is a Man*, New York: The Orion Press, 1959.

Levi, Primo, *The Drowned and the Saved*, New York: Simon & Schuster, 2017.

Levi, Primo, *Opere*, 2 volumes, ed. Marco Belpoliti, Turin: Einaudi, 2017.

Levinas, Emmanuel, 'Reflections on the Philosophy of Hitlerism', *Critical Inquiry*, 17, 1, Autumn 1990, pp. 62–71.

Levinas, Emmanuel, *Entre nous: essais sur le penser-à-l'autre*, Paris: Grasset, 2016.

Lipstadt, Deborah, *History on Trial: My Day in Court with a Holocaust Denier*, New York: HarperPerennial, 2008.

Lyotard, Jean-François, *Le différend*, Paris: Les Éditions de Minuit, 1983.

Mallmann, Klaus-Michael, and Martin Cüppers, *Halbmond und Hakenkreuz: Das Dritte Reich, die Araber und Palästina*, Darmstadt: Primus Verlag, 2014.

Margalit, Avishai, *The Ethics of Memory*, Cambridge, MA: Harvard University Press, 2002.

Marty, Éric, *Une querelle avec Alain Badiou, philosophe*, Paris: Gallimard, 2007.

Massenzio, Marcello, *Le Juif errant ou l'art de survivre*, Paris: Cerf, 2010.

Miccoli, Giovanni, 'Racines chrétiennes et contribution catholique à l'essor de l'antisémitisme politique', in *Antisémythes: l'image des Juifs entre culture et politique (1848–1939)*, ed. Marie-Anne Matard-Bonucci, Paris: École française de Rome, 2005, pp. 43–52.

Milner, Jean-Claude, *Les penchants criminels de l'Europe démocratique*, Paris: Verdier, 2003.
Nolte, Ernst, *Der europäische Bürgerkrieg 1917–1945: Nationalsozialismus und Bolschewismus*, Munich: Herbig, 2000.
Novick, Peter, *The Holocaust in American Life*, Boston: Houghton Mifflin Company, 1999.
Pisanty, Valentina, 'I negazionismi', in *Storia della Shoah*, Vol. I: *La crisi dell'Europa, lo sterminio degli ebrei e la memoria del XX secolo*, ed. Marina Cattaruzza, Marcello Flores, Simon Levis Sulam and Enzo Traverso, Turin: UTET, 2005.
Poliakov, Léon, *The Aryan Myth: A History of Racist and Nationalist Ideas in Europe*, New York: Barnes & Noble Books, 1996.
Ricœur, Paul, *Das Rätsel der Vergangenheit. Erinnern – Vergessen – Verzeihen*, Göttingen: Wallstein, 1998.
Ricœur, Paul, *Memory, History, Forgetting*, University of Chicago Press, 2010.
Robin, Régine, *La mémoire saturée*, Paris: Stock, 2003.
Rousso, Henry, 'La négation du génocide juif', *L'Histoire*, 106, 1987, pp. 76–9.
Rousso, Henry, *Le syndrome de Vichy de 1944 à nos jours*, Paris: Seuil, 1990.
Shermer, Michael, and Alex Grobman, *Denying History: Who Says the Holocaust Never Happened and Why Do They Say It?*, Berkeley: University of California Press, 2009.
Sofsky, Wolfgang, *The Order of Terror: The Concentration Camp*, Princeton University Press, 2013.
Taguieff, Pierre-André, *L'imaginaire du complot mondial: aspects d'un mythe moderne*, Paris: Éditions Mille et une nuits, 2006.
Taguieff, Pierre-André, *L'antisémitisme*, Paris: Presses universitaires de France, 2015.
Taguieff, Pierre-André, *Judéophobie: la dernière vague (2000–2018)*, Paris: Fayard, 2018.
Todorov, Tzvetan, *Hope and Memory: Lessons from the Twentieth Century*, Princeton University Press, 2016.
Traverso, Enzo, *Auschwitz e gli intellettuali: la Shoah nella cultura del dopoguerra*, Bologna: il Mulino, 2004.
Trigano, Shmuel, *Les frontières de Auschwitz*, Paris: Le Livre de Poche, 2005.
Venezia, Shlomo, *Inside the Gas Chambers: Eight Months in the Sonderkommando of Auschwitz*, Cambridge: Polity, 2009.
Vercelli, Claudio, *Il negazionismo: storia di una menzogna*, Bari: Laterza, 2016.
Vidal-Naquet, Pierre, *Assassins of Memory*, New York: Columbia University Press, 1993.

Volkov, Shulamit, *Germans, Jews and Antisemites: Trials in Emancipation*, Cambridge University Press, 2006.

Wellers, Georges, *Les chambres à gaz ont existé: des documents, des témoignages, des chiffres*, Paris: Gallimard, 1981.

Wistrich, Robert S., *A Lethal Obsession: Anti-Semitism from Antiquity to the Global Jihad*, New York: Random House, 2010.

Yakira, Elhanan, *Post-sionisme, post-Shoah: trois essais sur une négation, une délégitimation et une diabolisation d'Israël*, Paris: Presses universitaires de France, 2010.